Praise for Naked

How is your spiritual walk with God? Are you living the victorious, abundant life that Jesus talks about in John 10:10? If not, this book is for you like it was for me! Toni has written a handbook, of sorts, filled with steps to follow that will open eyes to the fact that we are all called to be warriors. Once we determine who's army we are in, then she will show us through the Word of God how to mature in Christ and have that abundant life we all desire. This book shares experiences and victory over negative situations that will encourage you, and through God's Word will empower you to walk in the fullness of God. I see a Ladies Bible Study coming out of this book!

— Janey Hays
Executive Pastor
Sanctuary OK

Never Meet the Devil Naked is a practical tool for incorporating the Armor of God into your life…not just when you feel like you need it, but every minute of every day. Toni's candor about her own spiritual development will encourage believers of all ages and backgrounds. Whether you've been a follower of Christ for a day or many decades, you will find insight and motivation to take hold of everything the Word of God has for you to fight and win the battles in your life.

— Samantha Votaw
Associate Pastor
Victory Church OKC

Never Meet the Devil Naked

IF THERE'S NO WARRIOR WITHIN, THERE'S NO WARRIOR IN YOUR ARMOR.

TONI CHISM

WARRIOR HOUSE
PUBLISHING

Unless otherwise indicated, all scriptural quotations marked and referred to are from the *New King James Version* of the Bible.

Scripture quotations marked and referred to and marked NKJV: Scripture taken from the New King James Version®. Copyright © 1982 by Thomas Nelson. Used by permission. All rights reserved.

Scripture quotations referred to and marked AMPC: Scripture quotations marked (AMPC) are taken from the Amplified Bible, Copyright © 1954, 1958, 1962, 1964, 1965, 1987 by The Lockman Foundation. Used by permission.

Scripture quotations marked (TLB) are taken from The Living Bible copyright © 1971. Used by permission of Tyndale House Publishers, Carol Stream, Illinois 60188. All rights reserved.

Scripture quotations marked KJV are taken from the *King James Version* of the Bible.

Italics and bold used in Scripture passages are the author's own emphasis.

—

ISBN: 979-8-9852861-0-6 (paperback), 979-8-9852861-1-3 (e-book)

Never Meet the Devil Naked: If There's No Warrior Within, There's No Warrior in Your Armor

Subjects: Spiritual Warfare, Christian Living

Copyright © 2022 by Toni Chism, LLC

Published by Warrior House Publishing, Newcastle, OK 73065

www.tonichism.com

Cover Design, Text Design and Formatting: Writing Momentum LLC

Printed in the United States of America. All rights reserved. No portions of the book may be reproduced, stored in a retrieval system, or transmitted in any form or by any means—electronic, mechanical, recording, photocopy, scanning, or other—with the exception for brief quotations in critical reviews or articles, without the prior written permission of the publisher.

Contents

Free Study Guide   vii
Foreword   xi
Introduction for Guys   xiii

1. Daisy's Do   1
2. Be A Daisy   11
3. Building Core Strength   17
4. The Devil's Strategy   21
5. Our Coach, Apostle Paul   27
6. It Can Get Hot   33
7. In Christ   43
8. It's Supernatural   51
9. Visible And Invisible   61
10. The Walking Dead   71
11. The Warrior Within   81
12. Holy Spirit   95
13. Godliness   101
14. Seated In Power   107
15. Dear Daisy   117

Obtaining Your Armor   119
Clothed with Holy Spirit   121
Acknowledgments   125
Notes   127
About the Author   129
Spiritual Warfare is Not a Drill   131

My Gift to You

Hello warrior! You've purchased *Never Meet the Devil Naked* – now enjoy this FREE PDF study guide, normally $20, as my gift to you.

It's filled with interactive questions, reflections, and more ... all designed to help you develop your warrior spirit.

To download your free PDF study guide, simply go to:

ToniChism.com/studyguide

I dedicate this book to the One Who is always faithful. Thank You Jesus for all You've done for us. Thank You for teaching me, training me, and showing me how to live the abundant life You died to give. Thank You for never giving up on me. To God be the glory!

Foreword

An unseen battle is being waged around us every day. Now, more than ever, the world needs God's mature children, God's warriors of light, to stand up and take their place in the fight.

In *Never Meet the Devil Naked,* Toni Chism teaches us who we are in Christ and who He is in us. The Champion of Heaven is calling his daughters up higher and showing us that we are more than able to be victorious in this confrontation.

Throughout this spiritual coming-of-age book, Toni reveals the traits needed to emerge as a conqueror from every spiritual conflict. She explains in great detail, the importance of being a trained warrior, before we ever even attempt to enter the combat zone.

Spiritual battles are unavoidable, and they can be fierce. In this book Toni will show you how to fight like the warrior that God already says you are! We train to fight in the war, but the battle belongs to the Lord. These are powerful principles for men and women alike. This book is a must read for anyone desiring to be a culture-changer for the Kingdom of God.

Rebekah Cunningham
Pastor, Sanctuary OK
Co-founder, Crowned One Ministries

Introduction for Guys

Dear Men,

Just as God chose us and predestined us to adoption as sons by Jesus Christ to Himself, according to the good pleasure of His will (Ephesians 1:5), we know that includes His daughters.

Daughters are sons and sons are included in Christ as His brides.

While men aren't warrior daughters, men are warrior sons. Do what us gals do when we read the Scriptures. Know everything that is written, is written for sons and daughters. I hope you enjoy this book.

- Toni

CHAPTER 1

Daisy's Do

It was one of those moments that grab you from the beginning. The hour – high noon. The place—church. The ambience—peaceful, with lights dimmed to a soft glow. Me—as usual, I was in a rush.

Clipping across the distressed fibers of well-trodden carpet, I heard the sounds of teamwork. Women's voices, well above a whisper, were collaborating.

They'd gathered to pray for an upcoming women's event, and I intended to join them.

Their chatter wasn't gossip. Not at all. Breathless, rapid-fire words spilled over from one sentence to the next. It was important talk. Like a beautiful bouquet of daisies, the ladies painted the entryway with a rainbow of color as their conversation was directed at determining a clear strategy.

Full of joy and wearing flawless smiles, these daisies swayed to the rhythm of an unseen breeze. My arrival brought their attention. One charming, bright-eyed woman turned and gazed deep into my big browns. "Toni. Do you put your armor on when you get up in the morning?"

"I never take mine off," I answered.

"Oh," she said. Wonder seemed to flash across her face, and she said no more.

A woman next to her pressed her first and middle fingers against her lips and gazed into the distance. Priceless. They reminded me of—well, me.

HERE COMES THE PRACTICE

The group's bewildered expressions took me back to a time when I didn't understand how to keep my armor on. I presented a brave front. Dauntless, I was armed and ready to face whatever the devil threw my way.

I could pack a punch. I didn't like taking one, but I could throw one. I was a fighter thanks to my mother who'd groomed me to be the toughest kid on the block. But all this armor stuff was new to me.

Although I was a novice, I refused to live in fear. Good heavens. No. I'd learned to put the devil in his place by saying, "I bind you, Satan, in the Name of Jesus." I knew Psalm 91 and sang about dwelling in His Presence. I'd learned the phrase, *no fear here*, which I was faithful to shout every time anxiety confronted me.

While I may have talked the talk, I didn't know how to keep my armor on or how to use my weapons. I was also ignorant of the devil's devices. Lack of knowledge made me naked, ripe for Satan's pickings. I had more questions than answers. Questions like, where was all this invisible armor kept, and how did I put mine on?

I had no clue.

Worse, I didn't know the enemy sought out people who lived life with doors of least resistance. Doors that I had cracked open. I might as well have worn a top hat with a flashing neon sign that read, *Pick me, devil! Pick me!*

The truth was, I didn't know how to fight an invisible devil with invisible weapons in my invisible armor. That made me vulnerable and inadequate against the adversary's ploys.

I'd heard the armor training spiel. *The moment your feet hit the floor in the morning, apply each item of your armor. The practice of clothing oneself with the armor should become your habit. Then, and only then, will you be equipped for whatever the devil dishes out that day.*

It never worked that way for me. And although I didn't know much, I knew the One who had all the answers. So, I asked Him.

WET BEHIND THE EARS

During the early days of my warrior training, I tried to put my armor on in the morning. I wasn't sure yet what loins were, but I girded them. Wiping sleep from my eyes, I'd climb out of bed and say, "I gird my loins with truth! I put on the breastplate of righteousness! I shod my feet with preparation and the gospel of peace! I put on my helmet of salvation!"

In my imagination, I'd lift my shield of faith and say, "Take that devil!" as I slashed my invisible sword of the Spirit through the air. I was good with that invisible sword. I saw myself as a medieval white knight wielding a double-edge blade.

I only spoke the armor routine a few times because the process never felt quite right deep in the belly area, where my spirit was located.

"The spirit of man is the candle of the Lord, searching all the inward parts of the belly" (Proverbs 20:27 KJV).

The Lord, through His Spirit taught me a valuable lesson through an ordinary image. I learned that listening to His leading was like obeying a traffic signal. Sometimes the light was green which meant to keep on trucking. When Holy Spirit directed traffic, all was clear. If a possible collision lurked ahead, the light was yellow. A red light always meant stop! Danger was just around the corner.

Yellow lights were the most complicated to understand. Unlike my usual driving habit, they never meant hurry up and go faster before the light changed to red. Instead, I needed to slow down and listen for further leading.

Sometimes yellow meant prepare to stop. Or maybe there were obstacles ahead and I needed to proceed with caution. A yellow light could also mean that I should pray about the direction I was moving. Sometimes yellow just meant that the timing was off. Maybe I needed to stop and observe my surroundings.

I never liked the yellow lights, although they provided the most training. To either stop or go was rather easy. Well, it was easy after I'd learned to rein in my will. Sometimes submission was a challenge. But those yellow lights meant that I had to focus and pay close attention. I had to stay tuned-in to the Spirit.

Through the traffic light analogy, I learned Holy Spirit was the best teammate I could have. Since it was just the two of us, it was essential that I learned how to recognize His voice and direction. The faster I obeyed, the better. It took some hard knocks from the devil to learn that lesson. Eventually I got it and quit acting independently of Him.

Well, most of the time. Like everyone else, I was a work in progress.

I still am.

Over time, I learned that I was in control of the outcome. I could stop, look to the Lord to see what was going on, or ignore Holy Spirit's leading. Ignoring Him meant I would stop hearing Him call for my attention. I never wanted to quench Holy Spirit.

Little by little Holy Spirit brought me into a consistent, steady relationship with Him. Sirens didn't have to blare, and a shofar didn't need to blow for Him to get my attention. His gentle nudge, or check in my spirit, was enough. It was a sense of knowing that something wasn't right. The more I became aware of my spiritual nature, flowing with Him became as natural and unnoticed as breathing.

Reciting the armor speech felt uncomfortable, much like a red light illumined inside me. It left me gasping for breath, almost like a hyperventilation. Rapid breathing and anxiety set in much like the beginning of a panic attack. This all seemed to take place in my spirit.

I felt like I was trying to persuade myself into believing that I had my armor on. Heck, if I couldn't convince myself that I was wearing invisible armor, what kind of argument was I presenting to the devil?

TRAINING FOR BATTLE

I heard Kenneth E. Hagin, compare this uncomfortable sensation in his spirit to washing his feet with his socks on. I rushed home and tried it.

After filling the bathtub with water, I climbed in with only my knee socks on. I even soaped my socks up and waded around a bit. The feeling reminded me of jumping into Lake Michigan in jeans and a sweatshirt when I was a kid. Whether it was wet clothes or socks, they were clingy. They also weighed me down. I felt icky when I washed my feet with socks on. That icky feeling was Holy Spirit's way of letting me know that something wasn't right.

It was obvious I was going about this armor thing all wrong.

THE FAITH FIGHT

I learned a lot about battle from the Apostle Paul's trials and errors. God taught Paul how to keep his armor on and fight. Through the epistles, he explained how to stay dressed and ready for the good fight of faith. We had to be equipped for battle *before* donning the armor. I had to discover how to prepare myself with the confidence to stand when confronted by an invisible enemy. I learned confidence by following the Word of God and Holy Spirit's directions.

A BLANK SLATE

Other than a willing heart, I brought little to the table when I came to God. I wasn't raised in a church or in a family where I picked up information about the God life. He had to teach me everything.

I was tired of getting beat up and run over by the enemy Jesus defeated. Getting my clock cleaned by the devil taught me that verbally applying each piece of His armor was useless if I didn't learn the art of being a spiritual warrior. It wasn't about a verbal exercise; it was about staying prepared and ready.

TRACKING WITH THE SON

Every morning, daisies face east to greet the sun's rays. They so desire the sunlight that they turn their faces to follow the sun's path. God's beautiful women were created to track with the Son. Aligning with Him keeps us in His blessing and encompasses us with His protection.

It didn't take long to narrow down a few essentials. Especially if I didn't want to hear the enemy's petal game. "Does God love me? Or does He not?" I didn't need to put up with accusations, such as, *God said I was more than a conqueror, but*

I've lost a lot of battles. I thought I was healed. Except I'm still sick. God promised prosperity, but I'm always broke.

It was the proverbial snake whispering in my ear, "Did God really say…?"

In the beginning of my warrior training, the enemy had me plucking all the petals off my daisy. I hoped I'd end on the right answer when I reached the final petal. Playing that doubt and unbelief game cost me many battles.

The Apostle Paul knew what it felt like to lose a battle. He had to learn how to be a warrior in his armor, too. Under the direction of Holy Spirit, Paul taught me how to live prepared for battle so that I stay dressed in my armor. I learned to overcome obstacles by standing strong in the Lord and in the power of His might. The enemy ran roughshod over me until I learned this fact that began with knowing how to keep my armor on.

BEFORE THE ARMOR

Paul began with an all-important word, *finally,* in Ephesians 6:10. *Finally* can be defined as the last in a series of something related. It can also mean introducing a final point or reason.

Paul wrote in length about what it meant to be an overcoming warrior before describing our armor. "Finally, my brethren, be strong in the Lord and in the power of His might." Paul knew we needed strength to stand in our armor *before* putting on the whole armor of God.

"Put on the whole armor of God, that you may be able to **stand against the wiles of the devil**" (Ephesians 6:10-11 emphasis mine).

Paul wanted us to know that we weren't fighting the devil. That was news to me. Paul said we were to stand against the *wiles* of the devil. To stand against the wiles of the devil, we had to know how to keep our armor on.

Paul knew, as many of us have learned, if there was no warrior within, there would be no warrior in our armor. Armor or no armor, if we haven't acquired the skillset required to win, we won't. God will always be on our side, but we have a role in the battles we face in life.

Paul learned how to fight the good fight of faith so that he could be a warrior in his armor. I learned to do the same.

Let me address one misunderstanding. Some people believe that we're passive by-standers in this life of faith. After all, God is the one Who fights our battles. But if that were true, we wouldn't need armor. We wouldn't need a sword. We'd never see a Christian lose a battle to disease, die an early death, or live impoverished.

That's what this book is about. We do need to fight. It's a good fight and one that requires faith. But we need a warrior inside our armor. That way, we'll never lose another battle or face the devil naked.

Are you tired of losing battles? Are you fed-up with losing to the symptoms of sickness, disease, injury and lack? Would you like to learn how to be a warrior in your armor? If you're tired of meeting the devil naked, turn the page.

CHAPTER 2
Be A Daisy

In the late 1800s being called a *daisy* was all the rage. Daisies were never ordinary or wimpy. To call a woman a *daisy* meant she was a real doozy.

Doc Holliday, Wyatt Earp's dark and loyal friend, was the average nightmarish dentist of his day. Blood mingled with loud, Novocain-less, extraction screams were just part of what made him a dangerous man. Doc was rough, and always ready.

His dentistry practice suffered a devastating blow when excessive coughing from tuberculosis frightened his patients away. Perhaps it wasn't much of a stretch for a doozy in his boots to make. I mean, what fearless trail-blazin' dentist worth his salt wouldn't turn gun-slingin' gambler when forced to make a career change?

Doc's other loves beckoned him. Like the French card game, faro, by night, and prostitute and common-law wife, Big Nose Kate, by day. Legend has it that Doc was bad to the bone. Cocky and loaded with attitude, one-liners rolled off his tongue. "You're a daisy if you do!"

He incorporated the term *daisy* into his colorful personality and reputation. To the gunslinger Doc, if someone got the draw on him, they'd have to be pretty darn good. They'd be the best and fastest gun in the West. When Doc said, "You're no daisy. No daisy at all," he meant his opponent wasn't good enough to take him down. He was better on all counts.

THE DEVIL'S DAISY

Know from the beginning of this book that you're the devil's Daisy. The devil knows that, and you can, too.

As God's warrior daughter, you're not typical or ordinary in any way. With Christ in you, you can be the best and most marvelous at what you do. You may not have discovered your amazing daisy qualities yet, but the potential is within you.

Don't let the devil deceive you into believing otherwise. One of his favorite pastimes is taunting God's daughters with hurtful phrases like *not good enough*.

After spending millenniums in the presence of God's love, Satan's betrayal left him with a big hole on the inside that no amount of hate could fill. He still goes after those who don't know who they are in Christ.

Satan is anti-Christ, anti-God and antagonistic to our God-given identities. He provokes and wounds us to poison our confidence. His goal is to defeat us. When God's daughters have dry places within, he aims his darts to fill that void with vulnerability and inadequacy.

We're Satan's nemesis when we become a warrior on the inside of our armor. It's not the other way around. However, if we don't stay dressed in our armor, it's a very different story. With a very different ending.

Satan wants us to believe that he's the agent of our downfall. That couldn't be further from the truth, unless God's beautiful daisies don't know any better. Ignorance about who we are in Christ is deadly. As God's daughters, we can't allow Satan's agenda or those acting on his behalf to deceive us out of who God says that we are, or the possessions that He gave us.

MAKING HELL TREMBLE

God expects us to win against the devil's wiles. Jesus destroyed the power of the devil and put him under our feet. That's why we don't have to fight him. Because of Jesus, we stand against the devil's deceptive tricks, schemes, evil plots and strategies. All a Daisy needs to do is keep the pressure on him, so that he stays under her feet. That begins with knowledge.

Knowing that Jesus gave us His victory is the beginning. It's critical that we understand how to stand strong in the victory that Jesus died to give us. Our job is to keep the devil under our shodden feet by not giving him any place in our lives.

Shodden feet are "feet shod with the preparation of the gospel of peace," (Ephesians 6:15 KJV). It means that on purpose we bind peace to our hearts and to our minds so that our footing is solid and sure.

The Apostle Paul says, "And let the peace of God rule in your hearts…" (Colossians 3:15 KJV).

When we're at peace, we can rest assured of God's promises and protection. As warriors, we stand fast, and we stand strong against anything that attempts to steal our peace.

As God's warrior daughters, we must be confident that through Christ, we're enough to spoil the devil's schemes. We can't be unschooled or misinformed about what wearing our armor means. Not knowing how to stay dressed will get us run over.

If Doc came up against one of the devil's hounds, he'd scratch his pistol grip, look the dog straight in the eye and boldly declare, "You're no daisy. No daisy at all. But I'm here. And I'm your nightmare."

What gave Doc the audacity to take on every trigger-happy gunslinger that spit his chew near his feet? Where did Doc's bold confidence come from? With practice.

Like being quick and accurate on the draw, keeping the devil under our feet is an acquired skill. Standing strong in God's Word takes practice.

Opportunities will come and offer plenty of training. That's the nature of living in our world. Knowing how to win every battle is learned. But we have nothing to fear. God is on our side. And you, dear Daisy, are the gal for the job. Not in yourself, but in Christ. You have everything it takes to become a skilled warrior in your own armor.

TONI'S TAKE

"As newborn babes, desire the pure milk of the word, that you may grow" (1 Peter 2:2).

When my daughters were babies, they were passionate about their milk. They didn't care what time of the day or night it was. When they wanted to eat, they wanted to eat ten minutes ago. Their desire to eat was so strong I'd stop whatever I was doing and run to their rescue. Their need put a demand on me.

That's how God is with His babies.

When I surrendered my life to God, I craved after Him. Although I'd never seen a Bible for sale, I wanted one. One Saturday I discovered a booth full of Bibles at a flea market where I shopped. I bought one and began reading the Word of God. The more I read the Bible, the more I wanted to read. I had an intense desire to know God and what He had to say.

Grabbing my Bible, I'd light up a cigarette. I spent hours burning through a pack of smokes as I'd talk to God and soak up His Word. The pages were full of burn holes from the hot ash that dropped from cigarette tips.

I may have been addicted to smoking, but I craved spiritual milk. Paul through Holy Spirit, said that he fed the believers in Corinth, with milk.

"I fed you with milk and not with solid food…" (1 Corinthians 3:2).

Like us, God starts His babies with milk, not meat and potatoes. Babies can't handle solid food yet. Milk makes babies grow strong and healthy until pureed cereals, fruits and veggies can be introduced.

God nurtures and protects us in the same way. Just as we expect our children to stop whining, get their thumbs out of their mouths, and feed themselves, God likes His kids to grow-up also.

God introduced me to spiritual basics a little at a time. He didn't want me to choke or have intestinal nasties. Phew! As I grew, He began feeding me solid foods. He brought me from baby to spiritual warrior. Since I started out neck deep in the devil's poo, I had to be a quick study on warfare.

Thank God, He accepts us as we are. He invites us to drink His milk, eat from His table, and we don't have to clean up first. As I grew in the knowledge of God and in His ways, I learned to keep my armor on so that I walked as a warrior prepared for battle.

CHAPTER 3
Building Core Strength

Our core is far more than our stomach muscles. The core wraps from the front of our bodies, around the sides and includes the back. God gave us a system of muscles that need conditioning if we're going to protect our spine and keep our metabolism running at peak performance. In a similar way, we need a strong spiritual core to wear God's armor.

Standing strong against the devil's schemes requires tenacity or staying power. In the face of adversity when our bodies are tired and our emotions are drained, it's a strong spiritual backbone, not a wishbone, that supports our walk in Christ.

Building core spiritual muscles requires strength of character. When we know who we are in Christ we can't be talked out of our identity. We can know what belongs to us because we belong to God. Imprinting our minds and hearts with God's Word is essential. Knowing Truth fortifies our commitment to walk by His principles instead of our feelings or the enemy's lies.

The heart of the matter is what we believe at our core. These are our non-negotiable values that make us who we are. They're our deepest, anchored convictions about God, ourselves, others, and the world. Our goal is to see our belief system rooted in God's Truth. When it is, our thinking and conduct follow a sure path. The Bible guides how we process life and its challenges in the right way. We enter God's rest.

When we're grounded in God's Word and something comes to steal, kill, and destroy, our conviction shouts, "No way, devil! I'm a Blood-bought child of God. You take your thieving hands off me!"

Our response is quick when we know and have confidence in the Word. Jesus said, "The thief comes only to steal, and to kill, and to destroy. I have come that they may have life, and that they may have it more abundantly" (John 10:10).

We say, "Good God, Almighty! No weapon formed against me prospers. Thank You, Jesus!"

Agreement with God becomes our first line of defense when His Truth is ingrained into our very core. We won't give that devil a nano second of our thought process. When John 10:10 is rooted deeply into our belief system, we can take an immediate stand against the enemy's schemes.

Satan doesn't know what to do with a Daisy like that.

On the other hand, if we hesitate, are indecisive and perplexed, we're heading for a land mine. If we start wondering if the sickness we may be experiencing is from God, then add some whining, we've lost our spiritual footing. We won't be able to keep the devil under our manicured tootsies.

We take off the helmet of salvation when we wonder if God means what He says. That wondering causes us to lay down our shield of faith. Before long, we're almost naked and exposed to the fiery darts of the enemy.

Standing against the wiles of the devil means that we stake our claim on God's Truth. We fight the good fight of faith by refusing to budge from His faithfulness to His promise. The enemy does exactly what John 10:10 said. But God nullified every demonic design and offered abundance as His response.

Having a strong core enables us to latch onto God so that come hell or high water, we stand and fight the good fight of faith—and win. When we're fighting for the lives of those we love and for what legally belongs to us through the death, burial, and resurrection of our Jesus, we must be strong and never let go. Our feet must be so adhered to God's Truth that a grain of sand can't squeeze its way between. That means no blisters!

A strong core keeps us fixed and stable. A powerhouse in God's armor.

EXERCISE REQUIRED

Paul was our coach throughout much of the New Testament. He commanded his son in the faith, Timothy, in this way.

"…exercise yourself toward godliness. For bodily exercise profits a little, but godliness is profitable for all things, having promise of the life that now is and of that which is to come" (1 Timothy 4:7-8).

Paul's words still urge us as spiritual sons and daughters in the faith, to exercise ourselves in godliness. Godliness is how we walk out our righteous identity in Christ. Without godliness, we'd have a weak core, no backbone and leave ourselves open for enemy attack. Without godliness, we'd be naked.

CHAPTER 4
The Devil's Strategy

Paul prepared God's kids to become confident in their armor in the first five and a half chapters of Ephesians. He presented the fundamentals to apply before we put our armor on.

Warriors never entered battle without disciplining their minds and bodies for warfare. They never entered battle expecting to lose. God's warrior daughters shouldn't be any different. We should expect to win every battle.

In the Book of Ephesians, warriors learned their rank and position, who their enemy was, and the strategy for engagement.

Our enemy is a spirit. Our own strength with natural weapons will never be enough against this adversary. I had to read the Bible for myself and spend time with God, allowing Holy Spirit to teach me. That's how I became strong in the Lord.

"Finally, my brethren, be strong in the Lord and in the power of His might. Put on the whole armor of God, that you may be able to stand against the wiles of the devil" (Ephesians 6:10-11).

Whose armor are we to put on? God's armor. We need spiritual armor to stand against the wiles of a spiritual enemy.

WILES

According to my favorite Greek scholar, Rick Renner, the word *wiles* literally means *with a road*. Renner said, "…the enemy travels on one road, one lane, or one avenue. In other words, he primarily has only one trick in his bag…"[1]

According to Renner, there are two other words we need to understand. They are *devices* and *deception*.

DEVICES

"Lest Satan should get an advantage of us: for we are not ignorant of his devices" (2 Corinthians 2:11).

Renner said, "The word *devices* is taken from the word *noemata*, which is derived from the word *nous*. The word *nous* is the Greek word for the mind or intellect. However, the form *noemata*, as used by Paul in Second Corinthians 2:11, carries the idea of a *deceived mind*. Specifically, this word *noemata* denotes the insidious and malevolent plot of Satan to fill the human mind with *confusion*."[2]

The devil works in confusion. Once I started drinking the milk of the Word and gave my attention to God by reading the Bible, all that changed. Wisdom came. Confusion vanished. It wasn't instant. But little by little I was able to digest more than milk. I started understanding a few things. I went from sipping milk to knowing how to keep my armor on.

I connected my new ability to understand to Moses's burning bush experience.

Moses saw the bush that was burning but wasn't consumed. He said, "…I will now turn aside and see this great sight…" (Exodus 3:3).

He stopped what he was doing and turned his attention to God, giving Him room to speak. When the Lord saw that He had Moses's attention, He started speaking.

I didn't see a burning bush, but I stopped being so pre-occupied with other things and made room for God in my life. He hasn't stopped talking since.

DECEPTION

The third word Renner says we need to understand concerning *wiles* is the word *deception*.

"Deception occurs when a person believes the lies that the enemy has been telling him. The moment someone begins to accept Satan's lies as truth is the very moment those wicked thoughts and mind games begin to produce the devil's reality in his life."[3]

Once Satan lays a road into the mind, he attempts to deceive us with lies against the truth of God's Word.

For instance, the devil may attack your mind by whispering, "You'll never be able to keep your armor on. You've lost so many battles, you're a wimpy failure. You'll never live in the abundance Jesus died to give you. Abundance is a lie, anyway. Money is evil. You'll never get out of debt. Yes, God may heal some, but not you."

When you don't have first-hand knowledge of what God says, those lies cause confusion. When you know how to combat the devil's lies by replacing them with God's Truth, they won't have power in your life. You have to drink your milk!

MIGHTY MEN AND WOMEN OF VALOR

One way we can learn to stop the devil from paving a road into our thought lives is by observing how God trained the warriors of old. The Bible is full of examples of everyday people who did extraordinary things when they changed their thinking.

Gideon was a reluctant warrior at first. He faced his fears and quit hiding behind the winepress to become mighty in God. He destroyed a demonic altar dedicated to Baal and was listed in what's known as the Faith's Hall of Fame in Hebrews 11. Gideon fought the good fight of faith and won.

Like Gideon, the Apostle Paul had to change his thinking about who he was by accepting his identity in Christ. He gained an understanding about how to function in the kingdom of God and then taught others. Receiving our redeemed nature is an essential key to success in the kingdom of God.

Paul faced a host of challenges that were as fierce as lions and tigers and bears. He stood against an onslaught of demonic activity that gave him plenty of opportunity to practice. Like Paul and Gideon, we have a stint in boot-camp, too. We'll get plenty of on-the-job training as we adapt to our new spiritual mindset. Paul warned us.

"I know that after I'm gone, ferocious wolves will get in among you, not sparing the flock" (Acts 20:29 AMPC).

WOLVES

The purpose of a wolf in the spirit is to tear us apart. Wolves were never meant to be turned into cuddly, house-trained pets. Their nature is to turn and attack. For me, smoking cigarettes was an expensive wolf.

Paul understood that we couldn't live like the devil and expect to defeat him. He'd faced some wolves, himself. There were reasons that God chose Paul to teach us about spiritual warfare and how to keep our armor on.

CHAPTER 5
Our Coach, Apostle Paul

Each of us has a history. We come to God from different backgrounds, cultures, and perspectives. We enter the kingdom of God with unique motivations and grow at different rates. Some of us had colorful role models. Others were groomed by old souls and wholesome characters. Our unique backgrounds provide for a variety of belief systems. We have our own mix of addictions, likes, dislikes, and idiosyncrasies. Paul was no exception.

To put it mildly, Paul, formerly known as Saul, was quite the rascal.

As the son of a Pharisee, Saul considered himself the Pharisee of Pharisees. He was a mean, religious persecutor who hated and pursued Christians to their death. Saul thought he was doing God's work. He was a zealous man with grit, determination, and backbone.

Those are fine qualities with the right heart. But Saul's heart was full of hate. Like many of his contemporaries, he had an anti-Christ spirit that blinded his eyes to Jesus as the prophesied Messiah. He was a vicious adversary.

Saul and the gang he ran with were all anti-Christ. They opposed Christ, His teachings, and His followers. Backed by the Jewish leaders and the Roman government, Saul was ruthless against the Christians, known as followers of the Way.

Instead of embracing Christ's ways, Saul and his gang wanted to hold fast to their traditions and the letter of the law, which he later said would kill believers.

"[It is He] Who has qualified us [making us to be fit and worthy and sufficient] as ministers and dispensers of a new covenant [of salvation through Christ], not [ministers] of the letter (of legally written code) but of the Spirit; for the code [of the Law] kills, but the [Holy] Spirit makes alive" (2 Corinthians 3:6 AMPC).

SPIRITUAL REBIRTH

After persecuting and murdering Jesus's followers, in a blinding encounter with Jesus, the Lord of Glory, Saul turned from being a minister of religious law to proclaiming the new covenant of salvation through Jesus Christ. Saul had a change of heart. He saw *The* Light and lost his natural vision for a few days. This got his attention. He had to stop what he was doing and give God room to speak (Acts Chapter 9).

The experience made a believer out of him. When he regained his eyesight, he became a follower of the Way and one of the Lord's witnessing warriors.

Paul didn't begin his new Jesus-life knowing how to be successful in God's armor any more than we do. Paul had to grow up in the things of God just as we must.

When I first started reading about Paul in the New Testament, he seemed bigger than life. He was my Biblical superstar. What I began to understand, though, was that Paul was a human being like me. He lived out what he taught the church, empowered by Holy Spirit. He learned to talk the kingdom of God talk and he lived out what he believed. Paul became the apostle to the apostles, but he began just like you and I —as a babe in the God-life and in spiritual warfare.

Paul chose to be empowered and led by Holy Spirit after he received Jesus Christ as his Lord and Savior. That's a choice we must make, also. It's our decision to choose Jesus as our Savior. It's another decision altogether to choose Jesus as our Lord.

Once He is our Savior, choosing Jesus as Lord is an ongoing decision of our will. Each day we choose to follow what God says. Our obedience is proof of a new nature based in righteousness and truth.

NEW NATURE, NEW WAY OF LIVING

Paul lived during the days of both the Old and New Testaments, known as the Covenants, that God made with man.

He also lived during the transition period between the Covenants, when Jesus walked the earth as a man.

If there's a thing or two that I know about Paul, it's that he loved God and that he had a warrior spirit. As a master of Jewish law, Paul was an Old Testament scholar. He knew the stories of the faith heroes of old. He studied and was acquainted with the patriarchs, prophets, saints, and covenants. Paul knew the prophecies that foretold of Jesus's birth, life, and death. He was a well-educated man.

Me? When I began my new life with God, I didn't know anything about the Bible. I knew the Lord's Prayer, but I didn't know that it was in the Bible. I was Scripturally illiterate. I wouldn't say that I was fearless like Paul was, but I was a fighter. I still am.

LOCATING YOU

What about you? Where do you come from?

Maybe you're like I was—ignorant of God and His ways. I didn't understand that the devil was my enemy. I didn't even know that God loved me.

It's a great idea to have a spiritual warfare journal to record your victories and to learn from your defeats. Begin by locating yourself. Where are you in your warrior training today? Have you grown in the ways of the Lord since you believed? Where are you in your spiritual development? Babyhood? Childhood? Those awful teenage years? Or adulthood?

When has God shown Himself strong on your behalf? When have you walked fearless in faith and won the battle? Ask God to show you past victories that may have gone by unnoticed. Ask Him to open your eyes to His Truth.

What scriptures are part of your arsenal?

Ask God to help you debrief about the times when you lost a battle.

After you get a snapshot of where you are now, thank God in advance for all that He's going to teach you, and for all that He's already taught you. Give Him some praise and then sign and date your entry.

CHAPTER 6
It Can Get Hot

It would be a disservice to Paul not to look at some of his own testimonies. Although there shouldn't be, there's controversy in the church about Paul's experiences.

"Persecutions, afflictions, which happened to me at Antioch, at Iconium, at Lystra—which persecutions I endured. And out of them all the Lord delivered me" (2 Timothy 3:11).

Out of how many persecutions that Paul suffered did he say the Lord delivered him?

From all of them—that's how many—all of them.

Notice that Paul said that he was persecuted, not sick or diseased.

At the time Paul made his debut, if you weren't a Jew, you were a Gentile or in a third category called the Church. The church Paul was building were former Gentiles and Jews who chose to believe in Jesus.

I wouldn't dare judge the Apostle Paul, but it's possible that he missed God's will a bit. When he was fed up with the Jews opposing and abusing him, he said, "…From now on I will go to the Gentiles" (Acts 18:6).

Another time when the Jews refused to hear him and Barnabas concerning salvation through Jesus Christ, he said, "…behold, we turn to the Gentiles" (Acts 13:46).

Turning to the Gentiles sounded like wisdom to me. And Jesus did say that's what He called Paul to do (Acts 9:15).

HEADSTRONG?

Although warned to stay away from the Jews, Paul seemed determined to proclaim the Gospel of Jesus Christ to the Jewish people.

In Lystra, Paul got his head bashed in, was stoned, and left for dead—by the Jews. The disciples prayed, and God raised him to life (Acts 14:19-20). But his body had to heal from all the abuse.

Have you ever been punched in the eye with a fist, or hit with a baseball? Having rocks hurled at you by livid men would leave your mouth, nose and cheeks split open, bloody and swollen, and your eyes possibly blinded. Paul's eyes had to be badly injured after a stoning in which his adversaries believed they'd killed him. His body was bruised and broken all over.

That's some tough on-the-job training.

One thing I like about Paul, is that after God delivered him and brought him back to life, he didn't sit around licking his wounds, feeling sorry for himself.

Paul didn't let what looked like a defeat—defeat him. The next day, Paul, along with Barnabas, walked almost twenty miles to Derbe (Acts 14:19). He held a healing meeting after he arrived (Acts 14:20-21). That's my kind of guy. Paul was tough and he practiced what he preached.

"Therefore, submit to God. Resist the devil and he will flee from you" (James 4:7).

Paul wasn't about to let the enemy take him out of commission. Paul pressed on. He submitted to what God called him to do. He resisted what the devil brought against him, and he had to flee. That's why coach Paul has the credentials to tell us to forget what lies in our past and keep pressing on in Christ (Philippians 3:13-15).

It's also why Paul informs us that people are not our enemy. Like the Jews presented obstacles for Paul, people may be our problem, but the devil is our enemy.

"For we wrestle not against flesh and blood, but against principalities, against powers, against the rulers of the darkness of this world, against spiritual wickedness in high places" (Ephesians 6:12 KJV).

Paul tells us our real enemies are hosts, or spirits of wickedness before he tells us to put our armor on. "Therefore put on God's complete armor, that you may be able to resist and stand your ground..." (Ephesians 6: 13 AMPC).

Whenever the word "therefore" appears in the Bible, it's *there for* a reason. Therefore to successfully resist a spiritual adversary, we need God's armor and spiritual weapons.

Paul was prepared and his feet were shod with God's Truth. We must be on guard and prepared so that the devil doesn't trick us into submitting to something Jesus died to redeem us from. We're to submit to God and resist the devil so that he flees.

THORNS

Another time Paul said that he'd sought the Lord three times asking that He'd deliver him from a thorn in his flesh. Again, a needless controversy. Paul told us this thorn was a messenger of Satan.

"And lest I should be exalted above measure by the abundance of the revelations, a thorn in the flesh was given to me, a messenger of Satan to buffet me, lest I be exalted above measure" (2 Corinthians 12:7).

Who assigns messengers of Satan?

Satan does.

God doesn't employ rogue angels and demons. Based on the Word we can decide if what happened to Paul was an effort to bring life or death.

"The thief does not come except to steal, and to kill, and to destroy. I have come that they may have life, and that they may have it more abundantly" (John 10:10).

Paul taught what it meant to be both children of God, and warriors in life. As Paul learned, he educated and trained the Body of Christ in the art of strategic warfare against Satan and his hounds. Satan wanted to end him.

Spiros Zodhiates, says the word *buffet* means to *"rap with the fist."*[1] Satan struck against Paul in an effort to stop him. Paul described what he experienced as a thorn. Thorns in the flesh are delivered through people. Have you ever pricked your finger on a thorn? Or, has someone antagonized you so much that you called them a thorn in your side? A pain in the neck?

Just as the devil once used Paul's old nature to persecute Christians, he used people he could manipulate to harass Paul. We still see that happening in our world today.

The devil is our enemy. The people he uses may be our problem, but they are the devil's pawns. Like Paul before he met the Lord, they don't even know he's manipulating them because they've been deceived.

It was Satan, not God who attempted to stop Paul from completing the assignment that God gave him. God wanted him to bring revelations to the Body of Christ. And that's what he did, regardless of opposition. Paul had a lot of backbone both in the natural and in the spiritual. He had tenacity. He persevered. He grew and excelled in the art of spiritual warfare.

Paul learned how to keep that devil under his feet. It wasn't that God refused to deliver him. God taught Paul that through Jesus Christ, he had all the authority and the power needed to stop the devil himself. That's one of Paul's messages to the church.

God told Paul that His grace was enough (2 Corinthians 12:9). It took Paul three times to hear that God's grace was sufficient to overcome whatever was going on in his life. But he got it and then acted on his authority. Paul learned how to tap into God's grace, which is His power toward us. For that reason, Paul was qualified to teach us.

It doesn't have to take us three times because we have Paul's example. That's one reason why the devil has deceived the church into thinking that it wasn't God's will to help Paul with the thorn.

Paul learned firsthand who he was in Christ. He learned what belonged to him because he belonged to Christ. He was seated in heavenly realms in Christ. That qualified him to coach us today.

If we were looking for a body-building coach, we'd have a list of qualifications that aided our selection. We'd look for personality, experience, credentials, and commitment. God was no different when He chose Paul to help build His Body, the church, the Body of Jesus Christ. That includes you and me.

TONI'S TAKE

I lost many battles and got beat up a lot as I learned what it meant to have authority over the devil. In the natural I have a godmother. But I didn't have a spiritual godmother who taught me the ropes. It was the University of Hard Knocks for me.

Once I found out that I had a seat in Christ at the right hand of God, I had to learn how to stay in my seat. I didn't learn as quickly as Paul. For one thing, my mouth got me crosswise with the devil a lot. I discovered that not everyone wanted to hear about what God was teaching me or doing in my life. I could clear a room faster than the odor-able skunk, Pepe Le Pew.

One time as I prayed and praised God under my breath at the restaurant where I worked, someone threw an object that smacked me hard right across my mouth. It wasn't sharp, and it didn't cut me, but it stung. It got my attention. That was a targeted demonic attack against me for glorifying God. The demons controlling and manipulating the person who threw it, didn't like the pressure Holy Spirit put on them. The demonic underworld does not like the presence of God filling the atmosphere.

In my armor, wielding my sword from my seat of authority, I learned to operate in the deliverance power of God. Just like Paul learned. Just like you'll learn. We can do nothing about the devil in our own strength. Through experiences like being smacked in the mouth, I've learned how I open doors to the devil. One way is by placing myself in situations where I don't belong.

HE'S AFTER YOUR THINKING

Paul's own testimonies are examples of how crafty the devil is. Satan wants you to think that God didn't help Paul so don't expect He'll help you, either. That's a lie. God is for us. Paul discovered that God, through Jesus Christ had already provided for everything he needed.

Paul said he received the revelations of what he wrote in God's Word straight from Jesus. It was Satan who tried to stop him from telling the rest of us.

"For I neither received it from man, nor was I taught *it*, but *it* came through the revelation of Jesus Christ" (Galatians 1:12).

I receive revelation through reading God's Word. As God's kids, He'll give us all understanding of His Word.

Satan wanted Paul stopped. He wants to stop me from sharing with you and he wants to stop you from understanding. By causing confusion and creating doubt and unbelief in your mind about the character of God, Satan will strip you naked of your armor.

JOSHUA

Through Moses's leadership God led the children of Israel out of captivity. However, God needed a warrior to bring His kids, Abraham's descendants, into the Promised Land. Joshua was that man. He began with potential just like you and me.

It will take more than good leadership if you want your promised land of abundance, good health, and victory. There are plenty of wolves and giants in the land. With God, you can take them. It's through Christ living in us, and us remaining in Him, that we are *more than conquerors* (Romans 8:37).

Joshua knew there were some six-fingered giants standing between him and what God promised. He also knew that through His God, he and his mighty men could win. Joshua was full of faith, but he needed the key to success.

"This Book of the Law shall not depart from your mouth, but you shall meditate in it day and night, that you may observe to do according to all that is written in it. For then you will make your way prosperous, and then you will have good success" (Joshua 1:8).

Joshua led the children of Israel to possess the Promised Land by meditating in God's Word. Giving God my attention to scripture was how His Truth took root in me.

God instructed Joshua to be strong and courageous, not terrified or discouraged. That was because the Lord His God was with him everywhere he went (Joshua 1:9). Our strength comes from the same promise.

CHAPTER 7
In Christ

EPHESIANS, CHAPTER ONE

I discovered that I was somebody in Christ. I don't just mean somebody. I mean in Christ, I was Summmmm-Body. That was big news to a nobody who'd been neglected, abused, and shunned throughout her life. Like Paul, like you, I have a history. A past I was excited to discover I could walk away from.

Is there anything that you'd like to leave in the dust behind you?

There are phrases in the Bible that helped me learn about my new identity in Christ Jesus. Phrases like *in Him, before Him, to Himself, in the beloved* and *in Christ*. They give us a glimpse of several of what I call Paul's P's—power, position, possessions and potential. Paul's P's are sprinkled throughout the Epistles. The ones in Ephesians take us straight into the *dunamis* power of God.

POWER

The Greek word *dunamis*, is where we get our English word dynamite. Daisy, as God's warrior daughter, you're not just SummmmmBody. You, dear Daisy also have the potential to do life in the power of God.

There are many role models and leaders in the kingdom of God. As God's daughters we need moms, grandmothers, godmothers, big sisters, friends and coaches to mentor in the Body of Christ. God never called us to be mediocre. But we also need warriors like Joshua, to teach us how to possess our Promised Land.

POSITION, POSSESSIONS AND POTENTIAL

We receive our new identities and our position in Christ when we receive Jesus as our Savior. All the possessions that God bestowed on us become ours at the same time. However, unless we know how to access those benefits and privileges, they'll remain potential. That includes God's armor and the ability to be a warrior in that armor.

In the Book of Ephesians, Paul introduces himself as an apostle of Jesus Christ, chosen by God's divine will. He said he was writing to the saints and to the faithful in Christ Jesus (Ephesians 1:1). That includes you and me. Paul wrote,

"Blessed *be* the God and Father of our Lord Jesus Christ, who has blessed us with every **spiritual blessing** in the heavenly *places* **in Christ**, just as He **chose us in Him** before the foundation of the world, that we should be holy and without blame **before Him** in love" (Ephesians 1:3-4 emphasis mine).

SPIRITUAL BLESSING, SPIRITUAL REALM

As if Paul couldn't wait any longer, he jumped right in by telling the saints and the faithful that God has blessed every one of us with spiritual blessing. That was exciting news! I had no clue what it meant, but I was full of anticipation.

Thank God, He didn't leave me ignorant. If you don't know what being blessed with spiritual blessing means, He won't leave you ignorant either.

I combed through the New Testament and underlined all the references that told me who I was in Christ and what belonged to me because I belonged to Him.

These spiritual blessings were for all of God's kids and that included me. I couldn't contain my joy. Some people didn't appreciate hearing about all the spiritual good news I was learning, though. With a little smirk and eye roll, some nicknamed me, Saint Toni. Some ran the other way when they saw me heading in their direction.

I didn't grow up hearing the word *blessed*. It wasn't a word that entered my vocabulary or my thinking until I was an adult. Today, I hear people everywhere say, "Have a blessed day" or "Blessings."

I like to respond by saying, "I plan to." Then I tell them, "Be blessed." To me that sounds like the way Jesus and God would say it—with authority.

Now that we know we've been blessed, let's choose to be blessed. We can't live life afraid of the devil or the circumstances that confront us and be blessed at the same time.

ENTER THE SPIRITUAL REALM

With a little different emphasis, this Scripture deserves to be repeated.

"Blessed *be* the God and Father of our Lord Jesus Christ, **who has blessed us with every spiritual blessing in the heavenly *places* in Christ**, just as He chose us in Him before the foundation of the world, that we should be holy and without blame before Him in love," (Ephesians 1:3-4 emphasis mine).

The Amplified Classic Bible Version calls heavenly places, *heavenly realm!*

Yes, with an exclamation point! The heavenly realm is God's territory. I spent the first twenty-six years of my life not knowing that we could connect with God or have a relationship with Him. I didn't know that God always heard me when I recited the few prayers I'd memorized. It was breathtaking to find out that I could communicate with Him and have a relationship with Him. It was marvelous to discover that He'd blessed me, and that He loved me. Me! God loved Toni.

If you came from a background where you were treated less than others, I know you're shouting to high heaven like I did. Over time I've learned that the *blessing* meant empowerment to prosper. Having struggled along financially for much of my adult life, that was happy news. Being empowered to prosper echoed the Sermon on the Mount where Jesus said, "Blessed *are* the poor in spirit, for theirs is the kingdom of heaven (Matthew 5:3).

By not knowing that God loved me or that He'd empowered me to prosper, I was spiritually poor.

What's good news to a poor person? You don't have to live in poverty anymore. When you get your inward man built up in Him, and understand that God has blessed you, the devil won't be able to keep you poor in any area of your life again.

I've said this so many times over the years, "The first thing that I ever got thrilled about in my life was Jesus." I read the Bible with such anticipation. I even sensed Paul's longing for us to know everything God provided.

God blessed us and chose us before the foundation of the world. Before God created the world, He made the decision that He wanted us blessed. He provided everything we needed before mankind ever existed. Certainly, before we ever blew it and sinned.

This is a good place to take a *selah* moment. Selah means to pause, and let the Word of God soak in. When we take time to meditate and soak in the Word, like God told Joshua to do in Joshua 1:8, His Word sprouts on the inside of us and brings new knowledge and understanding.

Discovering I was blessed and empowered to prosper supercharged my hope and expectation. My life at the time looked the opposite of blessed and prosperous. God was so good, though. He never left me in lack. I believed what God said and took Him at His Word.

We receive everything from God the same way we receive Jesus as our Savior. By grace through faith. According to Romans 10:10, we believe and therefore we speak. We respond to God's grace—His blessing, through the spirit of faith. Blessing us was part of God's initial and original plan for man. As Paul points out in the next verse, so was redemption.

"In Him we have redemption through His blood, the forgiveness of sins, according to the riches of His grace which He made to abound toward us in all wisdom and prudence" (Romans 10:7 emphasis mine).

REDEMPTION

I never knew that you and I, and every person who ever lived was captured at birth and taken prisoner by the devil. Yes! Our enemy. An anointed Bible teacher I know uses the phrase, "Say yuck twice."[1] I love that phrase, and it fits!

I didn't realize that the devil was our enemy. Or that God's only begotten Son, Jesus, saved and redeemed us from the hand of the enemy. This was all new. I had no idea what Jesus had done for me. He did it for you, too.

Redemption is defined as, "Repurchase of captured goods or prisoners; the act of procuring the deliverance of persons or things from the possession and power of captors by the payment of an equivalent..."[2]

Let's come to a screeching halt for a moment so that we can selah the word, *repurchase*. *Re* as in *again*. Meaning that we once belonged to God. He went to great lengths to give us an opportunity to re-turn to Him.

Wow! Being redeemed was something to shout about. Or as Madea would say, "Hallelujer!"

Holy Spirit through Paul wanted us to know that redemption from the hand of the enemy is part of God's spiritual blessing and provision. Satan kidnapped mankind, but God, through Jesus, bought us back. Who knew? Not me.

Every blessing including God's armor, the authority and power that we walk in while we're on the earth is part of that redemption package. Everything Jesus gave His life to restore to us is received by grace through faith. We just believe.

"For by grace you have been saved through faith, and that not of yourselves; it is the gift of God" (Ephesians 2:8).

CHAPTER 8
It's Supernatural

Whenever the word spiritual is mentioned, many people think of the dark, spooky side of the supernatural realm. It does exist, or we wouldn't need armor. I learned that lesson the hard way.

Never toy around with the dark side. Demons grab and suck the life out of you. That happened to me a long time ago. I had no clue that what I was doing connected me with the devil or that it would bring death into my life. Witchcraft in any form is a wolf.

Thank God through Jesus, He rescued me from that world. He may have rescued you from the dark side as well. Take a moment and tell God thank You for whatever He's rescued you from.

As God's daughters, we shouldn't be more familiar with the dark side of the supernatural than we are with the spiritual realm where Light Himself dwells.

SPIRITUAL BLESSING

Every blessing God blessed us with is first found in the spiritual realm, in Christ. That was His plan before the foundation of the world and before we ever existed. In the dateless past when only the Godhead lived, He designed the world, as well as His plan to bless us and redeem us. All because He loves us.

"By faith we understand that the worlds were framed by the word of God, so that the things which are seen were not made of things which are visible" (Hebrews 11:3).

BEFORE THE WORLD

Before there were trees, water, the earth, and the fullness therein—God provided for everything we could ever need in His realm. That's His provision of grace. We access it with the spirit of faith. We believe, therefore we speak.

"And since we have the same spirit of faith, according to what is written, "I believed and therefor I spoke," we also believe and therefore speak" (2 Corinthians 4:13).

Believing and speaking is God's plan for receiving from Him. He designed us with the ability to take what we need from the spirit realm and bring it into where we live by believing and speaking.

When Adam turned mankind over to Satan, Adam lost that spiritual ability. From then on, he began to function more from the sense and intellect realm.

Adam and Eve's spiritual nature had been alive to God until they chose to listen to Satan. That's when the spiritual umbilical cord that connected them to God was severed. They had no choice but to teach their children natural tendencies and ways. Before Christ, we've all learned to do life that way.

Jesus got our spiritual ability back, which was God's original intention.

"For I am the Lord, I do not change…" (Malachi 3:6).

Adam and Eve's fall from glory didn't change God's mind or His plan. But for us to operate from His spiritual perspective, we have to retrain our thinking to live a new way. We can flow in the spirit *and* from our renewed intellect. Let's not forget, God gave us brains for a reason.

All the blessings God offers respond to the spirit of faith. Good health, healing and prosperity are His will and manifest in our lives when we tap into what His grace provided, through faith.

Paul tells us that even the faith to believe is a gift from God (Ephesians 2:8). This God kind of faith is not the natural kind that we use in our day-to-day activities. For instance, I believe my car will start in the morning. I have faith that the chair I'm sitting in as I type this manuscript won't collapse.

However, the spirit of faith is a gift that God gives us when we receive Jesus. It's the faith to believe all things are possible with God. With the help of His Word and Holy Spirit, we're responsible for growing and developing our faith.

FAITH

Faith is a substance which is tangible (Hebrews 11:1). It may be invisible, but it is matter. If we could look into the spirit realm, I believe we could see it. I know I can feel the force of faith at work.

Faith is our way of accepting God's grace. It's us believing that what God says is true. I've heard one mighty man of God, Andrew Wommack, say that faith is our positive response to God's grace.

Through faith, we respond to a spiritual God.

By faith we agree with God who has no limits. When we believe what God says, our faith pleases Him.

TRAINED IN FAITH

I am thankful God trained me in the way of faith. When I talk with Him, one of the things I tell Him is, "Your Word is good enough for me." I don't have to have proof of what He's promised. I live life with the attitude that all things are possible with God, and expectation.

I don't have to see God to know that He exists or to believe what He's promised. When I've asked for a new car, I begin thanking Him that the new car is mine. I see my car with spiritual eyes. I don't wait to see it in my garage before I believe He's supplied the car.

Jesus said, "whatever things," and a car is a thing. "Whatever things" I ask for in faith, I'm to believe that I've received them, and I will have them (Mark 11:24).

Jesus taught us how to pray the prayer of faith.

"For assuredly, I say to you, whoever **says** to this mountain, 'Be removed and be cast into the sea,' and **does not doubt in his heart**, **but believes** that those things he **says** will be done, **he will have whatever he says**" (Mark 11:23 emphasis mine).

That's the spirit of faith. We believe therefore we speak.

Jesus taught us to take God at His Word. We do have to apply some wisdom along with our requests. It's always a good idea that we first ask God, what things we should ask for, then listen for His answer. We train ourselves to listen for the green, yellow, or red lights.

This is the basic principle for keeping our armor on. We take God at His Word and believe what God said. Therefore, we can say, "I stay fully dressed in God's armor at all times. I'm wise to the devil's tricks. He's not going to catch me naked."

FAITH PLEASES GOD

Hebrews 11:6 says, "…without faith *it* is impossible to please *Him*, for he who comes to God must believe that He is, and *that* He is a rewarder of those who diligently seek Him."

God's blessing, such as His armor, a new car or healing become evident, when through faith we put a demand on what His grace has provided. It's by faith so that it might be by God's grace, and to His glory (Romans 4:16).

When we believe, we allow God to shower us with blessing. It's to God's glory, not our own. We can't take credit. All we did was take God at His Word. It pleases God to be on the giving end. Faith always pleases God.

TONI'S TAKE

I was desperate to move out of Oklahoma City at one time. John and I had just married, and I didn't care for his house or its location. I'd been living the faith life for a few years but had suffered a major defeat by the enemy.

That defeat left me frustrated. As a young child in the Lord, I didn't understand what I'm able to share with you now. I had some victories under my belt, but I was more potential than warrior. I didn't know how to use my shield of faith in every situation to quench the enemy's darts. I was living proof of what a lack of knowledge and refusal to heed Holy Spirit's warnings will do to someone's life.

I got naked. And the devil took advantage of me. I didn't know God's Word well enough to know I should have been resisting the devil. I thought I could live anyway I wanted. I became entangled with his temptations. I put myself in situations and acted with behaviors that didn't exhibit godliness.

As a baby, God always rushed to my rescue whenever I cried out to Him. There came a time when I had to grow up. I had to put childish things away and stop acting like a brat.

Things got rough, and my strength was waning. What devastated me was that I'd bought into a lie of the devil. He'd convinced me that I'd ticked God off. So instead of resisting the devil to make him flee, I hid from God.

As a mature Christian, I know better. We're not going to make God angry. He won't abandon us. Unfortunately, I thought I'd gotten myself into a place where God wouldn't help me. I gave up my faith stand. By the time I'd straightened up my behavior—which opened the door for the enemy to come in and wreck my life, it was too late.

I had a lot of staying power, but I'd chosen to live like the devil, and it cost me. My life wouldn't have taken such a direct hit if I hadn't been living by faith. People do land jobs and buy houses without faith. However, for me, God's grace had provided everything for me and my girls from the food we ate, to my job, our car, and the house we lived. I lost almost everything.

As God helped me rebuild, I asked Him, "Why do I have to believe for everything I get?"

"Because faith works," He said.

His answer was enough for me to adjust my attitude and get in faith for a new house, and that's what I did.

I wanted to lean on a wishbone instead of my spiritual backbone and faith training. I wanted to stay a forever baby. God's provision doesn't work that way. His way is by faith so that there's no mistake that the answer came through His grace.

I teach people how to use their faith because that's how God taught me to live. After my encounter with Jesus, God taught me how to build a life the right way, by His grace through faith. After I'd lost most everything, He helped me rebuild my life through His Word and by faith. Faith is an absolute for His warrior daughters.

Recently I've heard that giants don't build houses with eight-foot ceilings. If they did, they'd get tired of getting whacked in the head. Joking aside, when we take God at His Word, we become faith giants and there is no ceiling. Unwavering faith in God takes us soaring to new heights where there are no limits.

JUST BELIEVE

According to Jesus, our job is to believe (Mark 5:36). He said, if we believe all things are possible with God, (Mark 9:23) then all things would be possible to us (Matthew 19:26). Grace tapped by faith is what makes everything possible.

That includes keeping the devil under our feet. I don't just mean our natural feet when we stomp around the floor shouting, "Devil, you're under my feet."

We're seated in high heaven. If we can believe, we will enjoy the possessions waiting for us in the spirit realm that God planned before we were ever born. If not, they'll remain potential.

If you believe what God says, and act like what He says is true, there will be a warrior in your armor. With practice, you'll win any battle that comes your way.

WHY SPIRITUAL BLESSINGS?

We've read Ephesians 1:3, twice. It's key, so let's take a deeper look and let God's Word come alive. Warriors take a long soak and immerse themselves in Truth.

"Blessed *be* the God and Father of our Lord Jesus Christ, who has blessed us with every spiritual blessing in the heavenly *places* in Christ."

One reason they're spiritual blessings is because the Godhead is Spirit. Jesus said, "God *is* Spirit, and those who worship Him must worship in spirit and truth" (John 4:24).

Jesus didn't get a body of flesh until He was born of Mary. Yet the Bible tells us that He was with God in the beginning and existed before all things.

"God created man in His own image, in the image of God He created him; male and female He created them" (Genesis 1:27).

God didn't give Adam a body of flesh until eleven verses later in chapter 2, verse 7.

Since God is Spirit and man was made in His image, it's not a stretch to see that man is a spirit. We are spirit and we live in a body of flesh. Everything has its origin in the spirit. You and I included.

Your healing, your child's healing, the financial miracle you need, the restoration of your marriage, are all in the spiritual realm.

When God blessed us with every spiritual blessing in heavenly places in Christ, nothing natural or physical existed yet. He hadn't created the earth or the earth's heavenly hosts. He hadn't created man. Everything we can see in the natural realm came out of the spiritual. Every spiritual blessing comes straight from Father God.

CHAPTER 9
Visible And Invisible

"By faith we understand that the worlds were framed by the word of God, so that the things which are seen were not made of things which are visible" (Hebrews 11:3).

God told us in the Book of Hebrews that He made the worlds and everything in them out of things we can't see. He didn't say they were made by things that didn't exist. God made the worlds and everything therein, out of things invisible to our natural eyes.

That's supernatural. That's limitless. And powerful. Positionally, you and I are seated in Christ. By tapping into His grace, God made everything as possible to us, as He did for Jesus.

Even the computer and keyboard (things seen) I'm using came out of the spiritual. What was required to produce them, existed first in the spiritual. The healing we need, financial increase, and the faith to stay dressed in our armor all come out of the spiritual realm.

"We look not at the things which are seen, but at the things which are unseen; for the things which are visible are temporal [just brief and fleeting], but the things which are invisible are everlasting *and* imperishable" (2 Corinthians 4:18 AMPC).

If you can see it, it's temporary. All things that can be seen, can be changed by what's not seen in the unseen realm. Can you see cancer? Can you see the effects of lack? With God, all things seen are subject to change.

God tells us that we're to look at the things which are unseen, because the invisible is everlasting and imperishable. God is unseen.

If you're not jumping up and down in your seat, as they say in the deep south, your wood is wet.

KRYPTONITE

Staying dressed in our armor requires confidence in God. Satan knows that if he can get people to believe what's not true, like the world came into existence through evolution, he can stop potential warriors from emerging. The idea of evolution is rooted in man's rational knowledge and sense realms.

Satan, the deceiver, works in these territories. Questioning God's Truth in any area opens the door for the enemy to damage our positive faith response. That's what happened to me when I thought I'd made God angry. I lost my confidence in God's willingness to help me.

EYES AND EARS

How do we look at the things that are unseen?

With spiritual eyes. In the case of evolution, we choose to believe what God says instead of ideas and explanations that filter through our minds. How God created the world is recorded in Genesis chapter one. God spoke the world and the fullness therein into existence. From the beginning He modeled the prayer of faith that Jesus taught (Mark 11:23).

"In the beginning God created the heavens and the earth. The earth was without form, and void; and darkness was on the face of the deep, And the Spirit of God was hovering over the face of the waters Then God said, 'Let there be light' and there was light…" (Genesis 1:1-3).

The phrase, *God said*, is repeated throughout Genesis chapter one. God tells us what He created, how He created it and that it was good. God's warriors don't pick and choose what they will and will not believe.

We believe what God says, and act like we believe it. You may not be able to see your spiritual eyes, but you can look through them. Choosing to see with spiritual eyes and hearing with spiritual ears are godliness characteristics.

God gave us two sets of eyes and two sets of ears. We have both our natural, physical eyes and ears, and a set of spiritual eyes and ears. We need all eight.

Jesus addressed this in Mark 4:9, when He spoke to a large crowd. He commanded those with ears, to hear. In the natural, the people had ears and were listening to Him. But it was those who received what He said as living truth with the power to change their lives who had their spiritual ears open.

Paul also addressed spiritual eyes and ears. "...*their* ears are hard of hearing, and their eyes they have closed, lest they should see with *their* eyes and hear with *their* ears, lest they should understand with *their* hearts..." (Acts 28:27).

Notice that God doesn't close anyone's eyes or ears or stop anyone from understanding. It's a choice each of us makes. And yes, we all have two hearts.

HEART MATTERS

Paul knew we had four eyes, four ears and two hearts, but I'd never heard that. When we get to the heart of the matter, we're referring to the real you and the real me. Our heart is the center of who we are.

The Apostle Peter spoke of the hidden man of the heart. "...*let it* be the hidden man of the heart, in that which is not corruptible..." (1 Peter 3:4 KJV).

The heart that Peter and Paul referred to has to do with ability to understand. That's not our thumper that keeps our blood circulating. The heart that comprehends is the hidden man of the heart, which is the real spiritual you.

We're not going any deeper here about spiritual senses. Just enough to understand that we can't keep our spiritual armor on when we depend on looking, hearing, and understanding in the natural. The armor of God is spiritual, and we hear His commands with spiritual ears. We see the enemy with spiritual eyes. You, as His warrior daughter, understand with your spiritual heart that will never die.

FORGETTING, A GODLINESS CHARACTERISTIC

Like those who have gone before him, Paul said that he had to forget things in the past. For us, that may mean a few minutes ago, yesterday, or years ago.

Speaking of Moses, Hebrews 11:27 says, "By faith he forsook Egypt, not fearing the wrath of the king, for he endured as seeing Him who is invisible."

Moses walked away from Egypt and left his past behind. Yet forty years later, Moses, gained the strength to walk straight up to Pharaoh and declare God's edicts. That took courage. At that time, Pharaoh was the leader of the most powerful army in the world.

Moses stood face to face with Pharaoh by taking his eyes off the circumstances, off his past, and off what he could see to focus on the invisible God. He learned to see with spiritual eyes.

At the age of seventy-five, Abraham left Ur of the Chaldees to go to Canaan (Genesis 11:31-12:9). Abraham trusted the invisible God for a new life, and the promise for a baby that he and his wife Sarah, were unable to conceive. He trusted the invisible God for a child he had no hope of seeing. But God is a game changer for all who will believe. That's supernatural. That's living in the spirit.

James, John, and Peter abandoned fishing careers to follow Jesus (Mark 1:17,18). They left their businesses, income and their past behind to become witnesses of the invisible God (Acts 1:8). He rewarded their faith. They witnessed many healed and the dead raised to life. They witnessed supernatural increase and abundance.

It takes faith to forget the past and press forward to the high call of what belongs to us in Christ. We have to trust God with our future to forget the past. Without faith in the unseen One, we could find plenty of opportunities to return to what was comfortable and what we've been rescued from in Christ (Hebrews 11:15).

When someone keeps looking back, they can't move forward. Paul said, "…forgetting those things which are behind and reaching forward to those things which are ahead, I press toward the goal for the prize of the upward call of God in Christ Jesus (Philippians 3:13-14).

God said, "The righteous shall live by his faith (Habakkuk 2:4). His faith means our own faith, whether weak or strong. We don't live by anyone's faith but our own. The New Testament equivalent is Romans 1:17: "For in it the righteousness of God is revealed from faith to faith; as it is written, 'The just shall live by faith'."

To be a warrior in our armor, Paul tells us to focus on our identity. Anything else is deception and of the enemy. We must see ourselves the same way God sees us, "holy and without blame before Him in love," (Ephesians 1:4).

We choose to believe what the unseen God says. "… let God be true but every man a liar" (Romans 3:4).

Remember, we're looking at what we can't see. You may not see how you're "holy and without blame" but God can and does see you in that way through His eyes of love.

You may see yourself as insignificant, naked, and vulnerable. But that's not truth! Picture yourself in the Spirit as a mighty warrior in your armor. You're dressed to the nines. You're a daisy who kicks the devil's butt out of her business.

Our job is to believe what God says. Spiritual insight is a skill we learn in basic warrior training and fine tune throughout our lives. We can't focus on the many mistakes that we've made and still be spiritual. They may be visible to us and to others, but God chooses not to see them.

I like that, don't you?

GOD'S WORD

While we may not be able to see God with our natural eyes, we can read His Word. There will never be a warrior in our armor without knowing the Word of God for ourselves. We'll never be able to keep our armor on or be strong in the Lord without having a relationship with Him through His Word. Reading the Bible is the number one way we learn to recognize His voice.

"…Today, if you will hear His voice, do not harden your hearts" (Hebrews 4:7).

Who would harden your heart? You. Not God.

"For the word of God *is* living and powerful, and sharper than any two-edged sword, piercing even to the division of soul and spirit, and of joints and marrow, and is a discerner of the thoughts and intents of the heart" (Hebrews 4:12).

GOD LOVES US GIRLS

Listen to what the Bible says about the woman with the alabaster jar of oil who anointed Jesus's feet. She'd messed up so much that the Pharisees called her a wicked sinner. But Jesus loved her.

Jesus said, "Therefore I say to you, her sins, which *are* many, are forgiven, for she loved much. But to whom little is forgiven, *the same* loves little" (Luke 7:47).

To those of us who have been forgiven much, our love for Him runs deep.

Look what Jesus said to this warrior daughter. "Then he said to the woman, "Your faith has saved you. Go in peace."

She believed. And was saved.

GO IN PEACE

Jesus told the woman that no matter how evil her former lifestyle was, when she believed, grace had her back.

The word peace means *shalom*, nothing missing, nothing broken. When she got up from the feet of Jesus, she stood whole, without shame or reproach. That took backbone to stand tall among the men who scorned her. When God accepts you, who cares what others think? Other than for Jesus, we know there's no one perfect or sinless, including our accusers.

Forgiveness is one of the many benefits He blessed us with in spiritual places. God chose not to hold anything against us. Knowing we're forgiven gives us bold confidence in our armor. We don't play the devil's petal game. His taunts, lies and accusations don't get to us because we know who we are in Christ. Do accusations still hurt? Sometimes. But through God we can conquer those feelings.

The woman with the alabaster jar didn't dwell on what the religious leaders had to say about her. Entertaining what the devil dishes out is not the mark of a warrior. She picks herself back up when she falls short and believes what God says is true—He is faithful. She asks for forgiveness, puts it behind her and moves forward. By doing so, she decapitates the enemy.

A warrior also knows she must forgive others, and herself. Self-condemnation, rehearsing the past and refusing to forgive will causes us to lose battles. We must be committed to believe and do what God says—that's godliness in operation.

We have to learn to see ourselves as God sees us—loved, forgiven, holy, without blame in Him. We forgive others in the same way. Love is an essential part of our armor, the very essence of faith at work (Galatians 5:6).

CHAPTER 10
The Walking Dead

The walking dead. Nope, I'm not referring to a zombie apocalypse. The horror for the literal walking dead is far worse. Now that we understand that we're spirits, it's important to understand that spirits never die.

"Therefore, we do not lose heart. Even though our outward *man* is perishing, yet the inward man is being renewed day by day" (2 Corinthians 4:16).

Like Abraham, one day our bodies will die (Genesis 25:8). In ancient days, the saying that someone gave up the ghost was a way of saying they died. In Corinthians, Paul said that although our bodies are perishing, the real us—the inward man who is spirit, is being renewed. Our spirit will never die.

Being spiritually dead means that a person is separated from God. It doesn't mean ceasing to exist. Countless people walk among us who are the walking dead. They're spiritually dead because they're separated from God. In Ephesians 2:1, Paul said there was a spirit at work in the walking dead.

"And you *He made alive*, who were dead in trespasses and sins, in which you once walked according to the course of this world, according to the prince of the power of the air, the spirit who now works in the sons of disobedience, among whom also we all once conducted ourselves in the lusts of our flesh, fulfilling the desires of the flesh and of the mind, and were by nature children of wrath, just as the others" (Ephesians 2:1-4).

When we receive Jesus, the Life-giver, in less than a heartbeat, we're made alive. We transition from eternal death to eternal life. We all live in eternity right now. When our spirit leaves our body, where we spend eternity will have already been determined. We'll either go with our Father God, or the father of lies, Satan.

With love and compassion, and without compromise, Paul wants us to know that since we've gone from death to life, we no longer have to act like the walking dead. We have a choice. Before Christ, we all lived according to the dictates of what our flesh desired. We don't have to live that way any longer. There's a better way. Of course, that's a choice we each make.

But continuing to live life like the walking dead compromises a warrior's position. It can jeopardize our win. Walking as a son or daughter in disobedience will get us naked faster than a Vegas stripper. God will still love us. We'll go to heaven when we die. But we can't expect to defeat the devil when we live in his camp. We won't be prepared for warfare.

READY FOR BATTLE

God told us our enemy is Satan and his gang. That enemy wants to devour us just like a hungry lion wants to tear his next meal apart.

"Be sober, be vigilant; because your adversary the devil walks about like a roaring lion, seeking whom he may devour" (1 Peter 5:8).

May means *maybe*. The devil looks for someone that he may be able to destroy. Don't let that be you or your loved ones.

Peter continues by telling us how not to be devour-able. "Resist him, steadfast in the faith…" (1 Peter 5:9).

To resist him means to refuse to cooperate with the enemy. You'll never be a daisy if you choose to live on the devil's territory. All commitment to godliness requires is a decision. Decide to stay armored up and do what it takes to win every battle. This is your life.

"…I have set before you life and death, blessing and cursing; therefore, choose life that both you and your descendants may live; that you may love the LORD your God, that you may obey His voice, and that you may cling to Him, for He is your life and the length of your days…" (Deuteronomy 30:19-20).

God put the choice of life and death in our hands—not His. He even offers us the right option. "Choose life." When we do, we release life into our generations.

Satan plays for keeps. He doesn't come to make you sick and miserable. He comes to kill you. He doesn't want to drag your kids into the drug scene for just a little while. He wants to destroy your family forever. We must resist the devil and his ways. Not some of his ways—all of them. As Holy Spirit brings to our attention what those ways are, our choice determines the path.

Choose to be a faithful saint. Remain committed to God and His Word. And that my dear Daisy, is the battle that will take place in your mind. Either choose to walk in a way that leads to life or follow the ways of the enemy. When you win the battle in your mind, your flesh will quit fighting and will instead "fall in" and drill the enemy. Everything is easier when our flesh cooperates.

If God hadn't told us that Satan and his gang are our enemy, we'd all be victims of something we had no choice or control over. But God has warned us that we have an enemy. He's given us His armor and informed us of our enemy's strategy—that's warfare.

This war between light and darkness is man's longest running active war. Paul, led by Holy Spirit wants us to know how to win the battles we'll face during this war that won't end until Jesus returns.

For the record, there are no civilians in this war. You can't opt out. There are no demilitarized zones. We're all in this war and we are either on one side or the other. Choosing to live like the walking dead will cost you—like it cost me when I tried. No one can straddle the fence for very long.

Paul advised, urged, and warned us about spiritual warfare. He even begged God's people to stop living and acting like those on the enemy's team.

And dear Daisies, the truth of the matter is black and white.

Our eternal destination may still be with God, but when we play on the devil's team, we've submitted to him in some way. He has the world fooled into believing the wrong definition of what having *one hell of a time* means.

HELL

Hell is a place of darkness and constant torment. *One hell of a time* on earth includes sickness, disease, and poverty. It means feeling your body wrench in agony as cancer chews on it, one mouthful at a time. *One hell of a time* here on earth is watching your loved one suffer in pain with something you are helpless to stop. The list goes on and on.

That's why God sent Adam and Eve out of the Garden (Genesis 3:22-24). If they'd eaten from the Tree of Life in their fallen state, their bodies wouldn't have been able to die. They would have lived *one hell of a time*, for eternity. Thank God for His mercy.

Jesus redeemed us from the curse of living hell on earth. Thankfully, people who are suffering can die. Although they've been redeemed from sickness and disease, many Christians continue to put up with having *one hell of a time* in that area. Some don't understand how to receive everything Jesus died to give us such as the healing He provided at the cross.

The enemy deceives people into thinking they're having a good time when they buy into the walking dead's behavior and lifestyle that he's famous for offering. There may be pleasure for a while. Hebrews 11:25 says that there is pleasure in sin, but only for a season. That piper wants to be paid a high price. The party life—unholy sex, immoral lifestyles, mind altering drugs and evil of every kind leads to death.

But in literal hell, there will be no such pleasures going on. You won't be frolicking in the sun or kicking back with your feet propped, sipping the suds. No margaritas. No football. There won't be any partying and dancing in the streets.

God made hell for the fallen angels which includes Satan and his demons, not for man. The world we live in is the devil's world (1 Corinthians 4:4). When Jesus returns and locks him away, he won't oversee the conditions in hell. He'll be stuck there just like all those he deceived into taking that trip with him for their eternity. Which, by the way, will be never-ending misery. There won't even be any light in hell to play faro or poker. You'll never see the faces of those you once loved. You'll never again enjoy the touch of another person.

AN ATTITUDE OF HEART

Holy Spirit through Paul wanted us all to know that God made us spiritually alive together with Christ. He raised us from among the living dead by the same Spirit of life that raised Jesus Christ from the dead (Romans 8:11).

With that life, Holy Spirit helps us change how we live on earth. Holy Spirit leads us into godliness. But we'll never enjoy living in the power of God if we choose to walk like the living dead.

The more we learn how to cooperate with Him and operate in His power, the easier it is to stay dressed. God's power won't work for us if we're living like the devil. And that's where the rubber meets this road. That's one reason many Christians don't see the results God promised. Others are like how I started out, ignorant that He's promised us anything. At different times in my life, I fit both categories. I had to grow up in some areas and stop letting my flesh dictate my behavior.

We made the right choice when we changed our eternal destination. Now we need to change the course we're living here on earth. I didn't know that when I received Jesus. That information may not have reached you either. But now that you know, you have a choice to make.

TONI'S TAKE

One time I was so angry at someone that I punched them in the eye as hard as I could. I broke my hand. Did that person deserve being punched? In my carnal, childish opinion they deserved to have both eyes blackened. But that didn't make me right. I acted out of my flesh. While his black eye went away quickly, I had six weeks in a cast clear up to my elbow.

We've been given the power for living a blessed, abundant life. But for that power to work on our behalf we must grow up and put childish things behind us (1 Corinthians 13:11).

I had to grow up in Christ. But for me to do that, I had to know what I was supposed to look like all grown up. That lifestyle had never been modeled to me.

Would you hand the keys to a Ferrari over to a five-year-old? Neither would God. How about letting a two-year-old play with fire? While we may be mature for our natural age, spiritual maturity is something different altogether.

After telling us about some of the gifts that God gave us that will help us mature, Paul wrote, "...we should no longer be children...but speaking the truth in love, may grow up in all things into Him" (Ephesians 4:14-15).

We need to stop acting like children and grow up spiritually to keep our armor on. Unless we want Satan to devour us.

SPIRITUAL WARRIORS

When you were in your mother's womb, she shared her body with you. She nourished you so that you'd grow strong and healthy. She also gave you your natural birthday. When you're born again in Christ, God gave you a spiritual birthday. Among your many birthday gifts, you're seated with Him in heavenly places. Accepting your seat is a godly decision. You believe what God says. You are who God says you are and nothing that He doesn't.

One of the many possessions and benefits you gained at your spiritual birth is the ability to understand spiritual things. The moment you were born-again of God, is the moment He gave you a new heart, and opened your spiritual eyes and ears. From then on, just as with your natural eyes and ears, you choose when to open them and when to close them.

Remember in Ephesians 1:22, God said that He put all things, in every realm, under Jesus's feet and made them subject to Him. That's why everything in every realm is subject to you. You're seated in Him, but enjoying those benefits are not automatic. They are potential. God delegating His power into our hands takes spiritual maturity and faith. He doesn't want a bunch of brats running around calling fire down to devour someone who ticked them off in a moment of road rage. Or breaking their hand because they punched someone. That's why Paul instructed us to grow up and walk in love toward others.

Paul had to grow up. Me? I'm still maturing. But I haven't punched anyone lately.

All things being under your feet includes Satan and every hound of hell. It includes sickness, disease, malfunction, lack and poverty of every kind. We don't have to put up with hell on earth.

When you're born-again you're seated with Him in the spiritual realm, where by faith, you can grab hold of whatever you need, and draw it into the natural.

THRONE ROOM RIGHTS

Prior to Christ's Passion, the disciples argued over who'd be the greatest among them (Luke 9:46). Sounds like immature kid stuff, right?

The disciples wanted rights and privileges. They wanted respect and clout. They wanted positions of honor. Even more, they wanted what Jesus had. They wanted influence and the ability to operate in the power of Holy Spirit that they witnessed in Jesus. They wanted the potential they sensed.

The mother of the Zebedee boys got on her knees before Jesus and requested that her two sons sit, one on His right side, and the other on His left side (Matthew 20:20-28). Jesus said those positions weren't His to grant.

Through God's grace in Christ, God gave us a position of authority and power at His right hand in Christ. Not only to do the works of Jesus, but to do even greater works (John 14:12). Jesus said we'd be His witnesses and receive power (Acts 1:8). The coveted seat at the right hand of God, in Christ and its power has been given to you (Ephesians 1:20). God said so. Don't argue with God, ask for understanding.

Satan fears that power. If he can keep us from growing up spiritually, he has nothing to fear.

CHAPTER 11
The Warrior Within

A paper tiger is someone who boasts of strength, or who appears to be powerful and threatening. On the inside, they're weak and ineffective. They don't have the grit it takes to stand. It's like a guard dog who barks a lot but doesn't protect the family. When danger rears its ugly head, he tucks his tail and runs away. Due to a lack of knowledge or discipline, many Christians are like paper tigers.

Some may not understand what's resident on the inside of them. Others haven't taken the time to develop and train their spirit. As God's warrior daughters, we must understand that we've been designed to win.

TRAINING

God trained Joshua, Paul, and me. He trained many of my friends and all the spiritual giants of our day. He's trained every daisy I know. Let God train you. When I was learning about the warrior within, I heard Kenneth Copeland say, "When you're in God's armor, Satan doesn't know if that's you, or Jesus in there."

Your armor isn't any ordinary armor. When you stand against the wiles of the devil, the hounds of hell won't be able to see who is inside your armor unless you expose yourself. You may be shaking in your shodden shoes, but the enemy won't know it, unless you speak contrary to the Word of faith.

"Though we walk in the flesh, we do not war according to the flesh. For the weapons of our warfare are not carnal but mighty in God for pulling down strongholds, casting down arguments and every high thing that exalts itself against the knowledge of God, bringing every thought into captivity to the obedience of Christ" (2 Corinthians 10:3-5).

You don't scare the devil. What terrifies the enemy and makes him tremble is when you understand how-to walk-in God's power. You become a threat when you understand how to stay armored-up and wield the Sword of the Spirit. Until then, you're only full of potential.

TONI'S TAKE

Training is never easy. Knowledge is never automatic. Skill is never attained without practice. You can do this. Through Christ you can do all things.

THE BATTLEFIELD

Paul tells us that the way we do warfare, isn't with weapons of the flesh. Our weapons are spiritual.

"For the weapons of our warfare are not carnal but mighty in God for pulling down **strongholds**, casting down arguments and every high thing that exalts itself against the knowledge of God, bringing every **thought** into captivity to the obedience of Christ" (2 Corinthians 10:4-5 emphasis mine).

When Paul tells us we're to cast down arguments and bring thoughts into captivity to the obedience of Christ, he's saying that our minds are Satan's battlefield of choice.

STRONGHOLDS AND THOUGHTS

Rick Renner wrote, "The *strongholds* Paul refers to are lies that the devil has ingrained so deeply in your mind and in your belief system that they now exert power over certain areas of your life."[1]

What exerts power over your will? Over your thinking? Limiting my pizza intake was tough but I won. I fought against nicotine and won. Over the years I've fought sickness and disease and won. I beat COVID-19. I knew Jesus died so that I didn't have to suffer with any kind of disease. Practicing God's Truth made my odds of overcoming the disease greater than the argument the medical field and the news media presented.

It was my job to bring every thought that contradicted God's Word captive and obedient to Christ. I could not allow anything that lied against God's Truth which said, by Jesus's stripes I was healed (1 Peter 2:24) to stand. I could not allow any thought contrary to what God said exert power in my life. Therefore, I fought the fight of faith from the position and understanding that if I was healed, then I am healed.

I was already keeping my immune system boosted when COVID attacked my body with symptoms. I used spiritual weapons against the symptoms and their root which was COVID-19. I took authority over COVID from my seated position of authority in Christ with words. My words of agreement with what God said.

I believe that by the stripes of Jesus I was healed at the cross according to Isaiah 53:4-5 and 1 Peter 2:24. I took a faith stand and COVID backed off. You can go to my website and download, *Here's Your Proof*, four Scriptures that prove God's will is always healing.

Anytime I'm fighting the good fight of faith, I pray and ask God for wisdom. I do my own homework and research. I listen for the green, yellow or red light within, and I make choices which often include natural weapons that are available and will help my body.

I categorize every sickness and disease as something that comes only to steal to kill and to destroy. That's the devil's mode of operation. That's spiritual. We can't fight spiritual battles without spiritual weapons.

God made us spirit, soul, and body. All three parts of us need care. God gave us doctors who fight alongside of us against the wiles of the devil. I fight to win. I'm not opposed to utilizing everything available that Holy Spirit gives me a green light to employ. But I layer all that I do with the Word of God first, and throughout the process.

Taking a faith stand isn't limited to sickness and disease. Faith in what God says is for every area of our lives. Some people battle the desire for sex, drugs, and alcohol. While these things manifest as problem areas in our lives, Satan is our enemy and he's behind the problem.

God's Word must be ingrained in our minds and in our hearts so we can release His Word from our mouths as naturally as breathing.

WORDS ARE SPIRITUAL WEAPONS

We'll take a deep dive into each piece of the spiritual armor God gave us in Book Two of this series titled, *Never Meet the Devil Half Naked*. Words are warfare weapons.

"For the weapons of our warfare are not physical [weapons of flesh and blood], but they are mighty before God for the overthrow *and* destruction of strongholds, [Inasmuch as we] refute arguments *and* theories *and* reasonings and every proud *and* lofty thing that sets itself up against the [true] knowledge of God; and we lead every thought *and* purpose away captive into the obedience of Christ (the Messiah, the Anointed One)" (2 Corinthians 10:4-5 AMPC).

Our weapons aren't of this world—they're spiritual. We can't see them. Our words are spiritual weapons. God says let the weak say I am strong (Joel 3:10).

God wasn't telling us to lie. He was telling us to use our words and agree with what He says about us. That's faith at work. We believe what God says and therefore we speak. That's why we need to know what God says. We don't want to lie against the Truth. That's a big oops.

Learning how to lead every thought and purpose that's contrary to God's thoughts and purposes for us, captive, is a skill. If it's contrary to what God says, it's of the wrong spirit.

We can't allow thoughts that contradict God to run amok in our thought life. Thoughts become words. We have to put down every argument and vain imagination that pops into our minds. If Satan can defeat us in our minds, he can defeat us in life. We won't be a daisy.

The way to take renegade thoughts captive is by replacing them with God's Word. When Satan puts a thought in your head that suggests, "You'll always be a loser." We choose to agree with what God says instead. It doesn't matter how we feel about it, we choose to agree with God, and say, "I am in Christ and through Christ living in me, I am more than a conqueror (Romans 8:37). I am well able to keep God's armor on. Jesus gave me the victory. I am strong in the Lord and in the power of His might (Ephesians 6:10). I win, I win, I win."

Daisy, did you see that by speaking words, you were fighting the good fight of faith? That's the spirit of faith rising. We're exercising ourselves toward godliness.

We may have two sets of eyes, ears, and hearts, but we have one tongue. Both our flesh and our spirit share our tongue.

We can choose words that come from the flesh, which is carnal and brings death, or we can submit our tongues to our spirit and agree with what God says. Agreeing with God brings life.

Right there, dear Daisy, is a secret to abundant life. Using our words to agree with what God says about us is a warfare strategy. God's Word is a weapon.

WARRING IN THE SPIRIT

To be a warrior in our armor, we must learn how to do warfare in the spirit. Choosing by faith to agree with what God says by using our words is part of that battle. We must choose to fight with spiritual weapons, not fists. That doesn't mean if someone hauls off and pops us, we can't defend ourselves. We don't have to stand there and let someone pulverize us. We're not punching bags.

TONI'S TAKE

That's what I've taught my own daughters. They were never to start a fight. However, they were not punching bags and they weren't expected just to stand there and let anyone beat on them either. I also taught them that the best defense isn't a block. The best defense was to not put themselves in situations that they're liable to get punched.

While we do live in this world, we don't have to hang out in the devil's lounge.

EYES WIDE OPEN

"And you *He made alive,* who were dead in trespasses and sins, in which you once walked according to the course of this world, according to the prince of the power of the air, the spirit who now works in the sons of disobedience."

Paul made a distinction between *trespass* and *sin.* Trespasses is translated from the Greek word *paraptoma,* which means a blunder. An oops.

Trespasses are the unintentional errors or blunders we all make. Acting in ignorance concerning God's Word can be an example of a blunder. It's unintentional when we don't know what God said. However, if we do know what God says and we disagree, it's a lie.

The Greek word for *sin* is *hamartia,* which refers to sin we commit when we know better. It means *missing the mark.* For example, stealing is sin. We know that. I used to frequent a decorator's store that had a sign in the bathroom that read, "Stealing is against man's law, and God's."

Isaiah prophesied of Jesus. He took all sickness and disease so that we could have health and healing for our body and peace for our mind. He became sin on our behalf and gave us His righteousness so that we could be free (Isaiah 53).

Isaiah 53:6 gives us the meaning of sin. "All of us, like sheep, have strayed away. We have left God's paths to follow our own…" (TLB). Leaving God's path to go our own way is sin.

We need to be well-acquainted with what God says. Reading the Bible with Holy Spirit's help is non-negotiable.

THE PRINCE AND POWER OF THE AIR

Satan and his hounds observe us. They watch our character. They know whether there's a warrior in our armor or if we're masquerading as one. When they see us living life Satan's way, we're no threat. Satan and his gang know God's Word. They know that God said we are what we think. Their strategy is to deceive us out of believing God's Truth.

"For as he thinks in his heart, so *is* he" (Proverbs 23:7).

Once we're made alive in Christ, Satan wants to prevent us from discovering the authority we have over him. When we know to be who we are in Christ, Satan knows we can stop demonic influence in our lives. One way he attempts to keep us ignorant and in the dark is to keep us thinking and living the way we lived before Christ.

He wants us to continue fulfilling the lusts of the flesh. The demonic underworld knows that our ability to receive from God, and the quality of our life depends on how we think. That's why he instigates opportunities. When we take his bait, sooner, rather than later, he'll catch us naked.

Paul wants us to know that before Jesus, we walked according to the prince of the power of the air. Having a sin nature, we were manipulated and controlled by the god of this world, Satan. Many who have received the free gift of salvation continue to live under the influence of this evil overlord. They become miserable Christians.

Before Christ they had no problem with their lifestyle. After receiving Christ, they experience distress, guilt, and condemnation because they sense Holy Spirit leading them away from their former habits into freedom. When they were unknowingly controlled by Satan, their conscience didn't convict them.

These people are what the Bible calls carnal Christians. They lack knowledge and don't understand what's going on. Generally, they stay unhappy and defeated until they renew their minds to God's Truth, knock off acting like the devil and grow up spiritually.

Once we're born-again our new spirit wants to walk in accordance with Holy Spirit. The Bible tells us how to do that. That's one reason dear Daisy, reading the Bible is non-negotiable.

THE LOVE AND FAITH WALK

Walk is from the Greek word *peripateo*. Definitions include *to tread all around, walk at large, to live, be occupied with.*

We should all ask, what are we occupied with? Are we walking in accordance with godliness?

Walking in the Spirit empowers us so that we do not fulfill the lusts of the flesh. Whether we walk in the Spirit, or according to the dictates of the flesh is a choice. That choice determines the power we walk in, the quality of our lives and whether we're able to keep our armor on.

Making the wrong choice is why many of God's kids fall prey to Satan. But remember, none of us walk perfectly or without missing the mark. Are we going to follow the things of the Spirit? Or are we going to follow the desires of the flesh? It's our decision to endeavor to do what's right that determines how we set our course. It's not that we do everything right and never make a mistake.

KINGDOM OF DARKNESS

Satan, the prince and power of the air, his demons and the angels who rebelled against God, fill the atmosphere that surrounds the earth. Anyone who hasn't been born-again of God, belongs to the spiritual kingdom of darkness.

The atmosphere around the earth is under heaven's domain where we're seated. To stay dressed we must remain in our seat, which is our place of authority. Positionally, we're above the satanic underworld and they are under our spiritual feet.

CAPTIVES

To varying degrees, Satan influences those under his power. Many people who haven't been born again would be called good and moral folks. That's because Adam and Eve ate from the tree of knowledge to know the difference between good and evil. Doing good doesn't mean you're born again.

We were called sinners because we had a sin nature not because of our behavior. Once we're born-again, what keeps us in bondage to satanic influence is thinking and conducting our lives in a way that opposes God's Word. Once we're born-again, we're no longer sinners because our nature has now become the righteousness of God in Christ (2 Corinthians 5:21).

God no longer treats us as sinners but as His own children. Until we make the decision to renew our minds to God's thoughts and ways, Satan will continue to rule and ride roughshod over our lives. He'll keep the upper hand even though we belong to God.

Many people will submit to certain behaviors but not to others. For instance, some people wouldn't dream of stealing but they lie or gossip. Gossip hurts the people God loves, and Jesus gave His life for. Anyone who submits their will to Satan comes under satanic influence and supports the satanic agenda. Big or small, a lot or a little.

ANGELS ON ASSIGNMENT

The angels who remained with God, fill the atmosphere as well. God's angels are on assignment as ministering spirits, and they're on our side (Hebrews 1:14). They want to get involved with our lives by helping us. God's angels exist in greater numbers than those who are against us. They listen for God's Word to be spoken (Psalm 103:20).

While God's intentions toward us are for good, Satan assigns his angels and demons for our harm.

The satanic underworld wants to keep God's kids unaware of the dangers that lurk when they're scantily dressed, with little or no spiritual armor. Demons like to sucker-punch those who are unschooled in Biblical truths. I lived in that state for many years.

Demonic entities taunt those who are untaught in the art of being God's warrior. They employ deceptive devises to keep the unenlightened bound. Their goal is to keep us ignorant, uninformed and defeated in life so they can achieve their purpose of stealing, killing and destroying.

While God has planned an abundant life for each of us, traveling Satan's path is doom and destruction. He can even get some Christians to accuse God of causing their problems. He influences their thinking by suggesting that God is trying to teach them something or keep them humbled.

Anytime we encounter demonic attacks, we have an arsenal to stop them in their tracks. The satanic underworld knows this. They know we've been given the authority to take them down.

When God's kids experience sickness, disease, lack or any part of the curse, it should be with the awareness that through Jesus Christ, we win. Jesus gave us His victory. A daisy chooses to win.

TONI'S TAKE

Remember when I talked about suffering a major defeat from the enemy? I was well-equipped but I'd lost my confidence. When I thought that I'd ticked God off, it was too much for my young self to handle.

I'd become involved in sexual sin. I refused to believe that sex outside of marriage was sin. I thought it was just another religious rule. The turning point came when I refused to honor the red-light Holy Spirit was flashing. I had plenty of time and opportunities to change my ways, but I'd refused.

Thinking I'd made God angry I watched my life crumble around me. I began wrestling with my flesh instead of casting down the fiery thoughts that the enemy used to pierce my mind. Thoughts like, *God gave me a chance and helped me build a life. I really blew it now.*

I didn't know what to do. I felt vulnerable and uncertain. I became carnal minded instead of operating in the spirit. I'd been deceived and left naked.

I didn't know yet that I could ask God to forgive me and get back on the right path. I didn't know yet that there was nothing I could do to stop Him from loving me or giving me a hundred life rebuilds.

When I finally admitted that Holy Spirit was trying to lead me into what would bring life, I'd already crashed. My loss was great, but it was only temporary. God restored abundantly more. And because of losing that battle, I recognize the enemy in that area. He'll never get me again.

As we learn and grow to maturity, we lose some battles. But it's in the heat of battle that warriors are made.

"To be carnally minded is death; but to be spiritually minded is life and peace" (Romans 8:6).

And that, beautiful Daisies, is key to staying dressed in God's armor.

CHAPTER 12

Holy Spirit

"Now to Him who is able to do exceedingly abundantly above all that we ask or think, according to the power that works in us" (Ephesians 3:20).

I think Tim Taylor, the Tool Man from the Home Improvement television show, would have been all over that verse. If there's one thing that we know about Tim, he likes power.

If God's ability to work on our behalf is according to the power that works "in us," then that means He put us in control of the power meter.

Does that mean God is not sovereign?

No. It means that God designed the system to work that way. And since God is sovereign, He's going to have His way.

I'll repeat what God said. God said that *He is able,* to do *exceedingly abundantly* on our behalf *according to the power that works in us.*

The Bible tells us that God is not a respecter of persons (Acts 10:34). God doesn't play favorites.

Could that be why some of God's kids receive healing and some don't? Could that be why some of God's kids walk in greater measures of financial prosperity while others live in lack?

No power at work on the inside of us means we're limiting God. When I lost confidence in my standing with God, I couldn't keep that fire power burning. When we have little or no power at work on the inside of us, there's little or no power at work on our behalf.

No power at work on the inside means there's no warrior within. If we don't have confidence in the truth of who He is and who we are in Him, we'll walk around naked and defeated.

God doesn't leave us ignorant of where this power comes from that works on our behalf. Coach Paul, operating by the power of Holy Spirit wrote this.

"May He grant you out of the rich treasury of His glory to be strengthened and reinforced with mighty power in the inner man by the [Holy] Spirit [Himself indwelling your innermost being and personality]" (Ephesians 3:16 AMPC).

After Jesus resurrected from the dead, He spent forty days teaching the disciples about the kingdom of God. He told the disciples to wait for His promise (Acts 1:3-4).

"But you shall receive power when the Holy Spirit has come upon you; and you shall be witnesses to Me in Jerusalem, and in all Judea and Samaria, and to the end of the earth" (Acts 1:3).

Witness of what? All His good works toward the children of men that He lavished on us before the foundation of the earth. Our lives should exhibit the blessing that Adam lost but that through our union with Christ Jesus, we got back.

Do you need healing in your body? Are your finances in a mess? How about your marriage? Do you know someone who needs healing or whose children have run amok?

GLAD YOU ASKED

Yes, when you're what the Bible calls born-again, Holy Spirit comes and dwells on the inside of you—no ifs, ands or doubt about it.

But wait! There's more.

Holy Spirit is a member of the Godhead. He is a Person, and He is a Presence. When Holy Spirit is in the room—you know it. Holy Spirit is Who the disciples heard about from Jesus.

"And behold, I will send forth **upon you** what My Father has promised; but remain in the city [Jerusalem] until you are **clothed with power** from on high" (Luke 24:49 AMPC emphasis mine).

Being clothed with power and being dressed in God's armor sound similar.

The power to stay dressed comes from—Holy Spirit. Being "clothed" with the power of Holy Spirit and having Him live on the inside of us are two very different things.

Instead of clothed with power, the New King James Version reads, "endued with power from on high."

That's what happened to Peter. He went from denying that he knew Jesus, not once, not twice, but three times (Luke 22:54-62) to becoming a powerful witness of God's lavish love for man. After Peter was clothed with power, even his shadow became empowered (Acts 5:15-16).

"And being assembled together with *them*, He commanded them not to depart from Jerusalem, but to wait for the Promise of the Father, 'which,' *He said,* 'you have heard from Me; for John truly baptized with water, but you shall be baptized with the Holy Spirit not many days from now'" (Acts 1:4-5).

When we believe the promise of the Father that comes after salvation, Holy Spirit comes upon us and clothes us with God's power. That's what opens the door for God's promise of signs and wonders (Mark 16:16-18).

Jesus made a distinction between John's baptism in water, and the baptism of Holy Spirit. They're not the same. John's baptism was a baptism of repentance (Acts 19:4). When we're baptized in water, we acknowledge that we've received Jesus as our Savior and recognize we're no longer sinners. Our nature was changed. We're now the righteousness of God in Christ and we have eternal life with the Father.

All baptism means is immersion. We can be immersed, or baptized in water, Holy Spirit, or coffee. We could be baptized or dipped in chocolate. Milk chocolate. Hopefully without nuts.

When we choose to be immersed in Holy Spirit, Jesus told the disciples what would happen. "But you shall receive power when the Holy Spirit has come upon you; and you shall be witnesses to Me in Jerusalem, and in all Judea and Samaria, and to the end of the earth" (Acts 1:8).

When the power of Holy Spirit comes upon us, we receive power to be His witnesses. We'll witness God's goodness, mercy, grace, and His healing power. Witnesses testify of what they've seen. To witness doesn't just mean to tell people that Jesus is the way to heaven.

As witnesses, Holy Spirit works through us like He worked through Jesus. Jesus saw many people healed with His own natural eyes. We have the same opportunity. As a man, Jesus always kept His armor on. Jesus walked in power. The devil didn't trick Him. Jesus grew to maturity. He grew from turning water into wine, to raising the dead.

OBEDIENCE TO THE WORD

The early church walked in power like Jesus walked in power. They were wholehearted in their commitment to God. The disciples, through the power of Holy Spirit, healed and restored people to health just like Jesus did.

That power is available to us today and the devil knows it. We must be clothed with Holy Spirit because it's His power that puts a stop to the enemy's works.

The power of Holy Spirit keeps us dressed and that doesn't happen without Him. Paul knew there was much for us to learn before putting on God's armor.

There's so much more to say about the empowerment of Holy Spirit. Ask Him to teach you about His armor. Ask Him to teach you about who He is. You won't regret it.

CHAPTER 13
Godliness

The reason I waited until the final section of this book to define godliness is because I didn't want it misunderstood. Godliness is more than a numbered list of dos and don'ts. External obedience was required in the Old Covenant. Under the New Covenant, godliness is a heart condition.

I heard a story about a little girl who was sent to sit in the corner for misbehaving. She sat with her arms crossed over her chest and said, "I may be sitting down on the outside, but I'm standing on the inside."

That's cute when a child says it. As an adult, it reflects an issue of the heart. The little girl obeyed her parents and sat in her chair in the corner. But her heart wasn't in it. God is all about our attitude.

In the Book of Matthew there's a story about a father who had two sons. He told the first son to go to work in the vineyard. The son refused but later had a change of heart. He repented and went to work in the vineyard as his father had asked.

The father asked his second son to go to work, and he said he'd go. However, this son did not go. Jesus asked the question, "Which of the two did the will of *his* father?" (Matthew 21:28-32)

That parable is a good example of heart condition. The first son may not have wanted to get up and get to work, but his heart wanted to do the right thing. The second son was a pretender.

Godliness isn't about doing everything perfect. Or, even wanting to do the right thing at first. Godliness is a heart choice that endeavors to do what's right in God's eyes. When we seek to honor Him with godly choices, we walk through this life well-armed.

Wrapping up his letter to the church, Paul writes, "Honor (esteem and value as precious) your father and your mother —this is the first commandment with a promise—That all may be well with you and that you may live long on the earth" (Ephesians 6:2-3 AMPC).

This applies to our natural parents. But it also applies to our Father God. Honoring our parents and honoring God yields a promise of long life on earth.

Reverent is the most common synonym for *godliness*. But first…

KING OF HEARTS

When we think of hearts, we often think of love. We may experience warm and cozy feelings from the affection we hold for those dear to us. Red hearts denote love and are a staple around Valentine's Day. We all understand what *I heart you*, means.

Hearts have a lot in common with godliness. We choose to love and show honor and worshipful reverence toward God. It's our attitude toward Him and the things that are important to Him.

Referring to our heart attitude toward God, Jesus put it this way. "But seek (aim at and strive after) first of all His kingdom and His righteousness (His way of doing and being right), and then all these things taken together will be given you besides" (Matthew 6:33 AMPC).

In the verses prior to this one, Jesus speaks of people who don't know God. They're anxious and worried about things that pertain to this life. Seeking God's way opens the door for His promises to be released.

Make no mistake, God wants things done His way. Expressing respect for God includes being kind to others. People are important to God. He sent His Son for all people, not just for those who would receive Him.

I've never heard any teaching about getting up in the morning and reciting Colossians 3:12-15, like many were taught to recite putting on their armor. I think if we practiced this scripture, we'd be better at staying dressed in our armor.

"Therefore, as *the* elect of God, holy and beloved, put on tender mercies, kindness, humility, meekness, longsuffering; bearing with one another, and forgiving one another, if anyone has a complaint against another; even as Christ forgave you, so you also *must* do. But above all these things put on love, which is the bond of perfection. And let the peace of God rule in your hearts…and be thankful…" (Colossians 3:12-15)

Paul said to *put on* these characteristics. I've found that when I put on these and other virtues that are sprinkled throughout the Word, I not only keep my armor on, but I also polish it. As a result, I shine.

Having been made in God's image we should respect ourselves and not let others take advantage or abuse us. We have to guard our heart against things that are disrespectful to God and harmful to us. Guarding our heart also keeps the door closed to the demonic underworld.

This isn't just to keep our armor in place, but because we love God back. Drawing a line between the things of God and that of the world establishes boundaries. We erect a wall between us and what steals, kills and destroys our lives.

HEART BEATS

Jesus didn't just pay a great price for others. He paid a tremendous price for me and you.

In my opinion, Jesus may have declared a boundary when he wrote in the sand. A woman who'd been caught in the very act of adultery was facing stoning by a mob. Her accusers asked Jesus to judge her. (John 8:1-11)

Jesus said that He came to save the world, not to judge the world (John 12:47). We're not to judge people either. When we're obedient to this godly virtue, we set ourselves up for success.

None of us will live the God-life perfectly. I didn't start my relationship with God fully trusting Him. His bigness was a little scary at first. Once I began spending time with Him, I grew to love Him. Loving Him isn't hard when we understand His true character—not the one that some religions portray.

God is truly good, and only good. He doesn't want any harm to come to us. His ways protect us. That's one reason He wants things done His way.

Eventually I found out that God loved me. I didn't know that at the beginning of our relationship. And you know what? He loves you too. He loves us as a kindhearted father loves his children.

From there, I grew to love God, others, and myself. I was on my way to becoming the daisy that I am today.

SIDING WITH GOD'S ENEMY

Satan is against us. Whether physically, mentally, or emotionally, Satan gets his jollies destroying people, especially Father's kids. He tries to snuff out godliness.

Whenever we side with the devil, it's disrespectful to Father God. In layman's terms, godliness means to be sold out to God.

As we've touched on throughout this book, godliness is a quality of our new-born again nature. Our spirit desires to be reverent and respectful to God. It's a force within that compels us to please our Heavenly Father.

Fidelity is another word that comes to mind that relates to godliness. Fidelity reflects our faithfulness to God like a magnifying glass. It's seen when we demonstrate loyalty toward Him, trust and belief in His Word, and when we support what He values by how we conduct our lives.

WEBSTER'S DICTIONARY

Noah Webster defined godliness as, *piety, belief in God and reverence for His character and laws.*[1]

He says, "Reverence is nearly equivalent to veneration…"[2] And that veneration is, "The highest degree of respect and reverence; respect mingled with some degree of awe; a feeling or sentiment excited by the dignity and superiority of a person, or by the sacredness of his character…"[3]

This sacredness of character can only be shared by the three who are One: our Father God, Jesus the Christ, and Holy Spirit.

CHAPTER 14
Seated In Power

God raised His kids up together and seated us, "Far above all principality, and power, and might, and dominion, and **every name that is named**, not only in this age but also in that which is to come" (Ephesians 1:21 emphasis mine).

Cancer is a name that has been named. Diabetes, Leukemia, COPD, organ malfunction, limb problems, arthritis, COVID-19 and all its variants are names. The list goes on and on. Those names are of the enemy. They're squatters without rights. God's kids have to kick them out.

Jesus said, "…all power is given unto me in heaven and in earth" (Matthew 28:18). We are seated in Him and have the same power and spiritual blessings available to us in Him.

Jesus said, "Behold, **I give unto you power** to tread on serpents and scorpions, and over all the power of the enemy: and nothing shall by any means hurt you" (Luke 10:19).

Who was given power over squatters?

You were, dear Daisy.

Serpents and scorpions are symbolic of the devil and his gang. As parents, we take steps to protect our children from harm and danger. God left nothing out of His protection plan for His kids.

"I therefore, the prisoner for the Lord, appeal to *and* beg you to walk (lead a life) worthy of the [divine] calling to which you have been called [with behavior that is a credit to the summons to God's service" (Ephesians 4:1 AMPC).

Did you catch the word *beg*? How about the word *summons*? Our coach, Paul, the mighty warrior, and apostle of apostles begs us to lead lives worthy of our position in Him. If we don't take the authority over the squatters, our full potential in never realized.

If we're going to live lives worthy of Him and wear our armor as a credit to God's service, we need to monitor our behavior. We're disrobing when we put on wrong behaviors, mindsets and bad attitudes. Ungodly decisions and attitudes create openings for the enemy to gain advantage over us. They quench Holy Spirit, the One with the power, and we become naked and vulnerable.

Since our natures have been changed from sinner to righteous in Christ, we no longer put up with being driven by the lusts of the flesh. We're not to be conformed to this world, and the way the world does things. We choose to be transformed by the entire renewal of our minds (Romans 12:2).

Without renewing our minds to the Truth of God's Word, we remain prisoners to the enemy. We might be saved, attend church, and pray, but to be warriors in our armor and obtain God's promises we need the power of God operating on the inside of us.

UNDER THE INFLUENCE

Most of us have seen children who've been affected by watching too much violence on television or from playing too many video games. Their behavior has been influenced by what they give their time and attention to.

Have you ever been around people who were under the influence of an 80-proof liquor? I grew up in bars and around people whose behaviors were altered by drinking.

In alcohol terms, the "proof" is the percentage of alcohol in the bottle times two. Whether it's 100 proof, or 80 proof, I know how people act who are under the influence. Maybe you know, too.

In spiritual terms, most of us can see the proof that someone is living under the influence of Satan. Like recognizing someone who indulges in hard liquor, we know what living life indulging the flesh looks like.

Marijuana, meth, and other drugs leave a trail of evidence, or proof of their existence. Habitual anger, hatred, bitterness, and strife are indicators of Satan's influence.

Living under the influence of Satan is woe, all right. It's the counterculture to God's original plan. It's a culture that the god of this world has influenced. Doing what feels good, baby, can get you and others killed. It'll leave you naked.

When the wrong lifestyle is the drug of choice, even toying around close to the riverbanks can take you under or have long reaching consequences. Eating the devil's mushrooms alters your mind. A single helping can change the course of your entire life for decades and even eternity.

However, we can choose to be under the influence of Holy Spirit. Before Christ comes into our lives, we were incapable of living the God life. In ourselves, few will ever realize the capacity or the power to overcome anything in a world manipulated by an evil overlord. For those who do manage to break the power of alcohol or drug abuse, pornography, and other addictions, without God, it's often only temporary.

Before Christ, many of us didn't even know the devil was a threat, let alone that he had a hand in our behaviors and the problems we encountered in life. That was too supernatural for many to believe. Outside of Jesus, Satan is the overlord, and he calls the shots. Without Jesus, Satan is a greater power and authority than a mere man.

TONI'S TAKE

I keep a pulse on my own life. You're a daisy if you do. A daisy isn't a daisy because she can stand strong against enemy attacks. A daisy is a daisy because she tracks with the Son. A daisy is strong in the Lord and in the power of His might. What enables a daisy to be the best and most marvelous and more than a conqueror, is because she's found in Him.

We all have standards that we've established. Saved or unsaved, the world pulls on all of us. Have you seen a movie advertised that you'd like to watch, only to discover its rated R? My husband John, and I have drawn a line. We don't watch R rated movies. Like checking the expiration dates on items at the supermarket, we've learned to check movie ratings.

Ever refrain from spouting off on social media? Me too. It's an area I need to do better. The standards we set guide our thoughts, our behaviors, our attitudes, mouths and set the course of our lives. The Bible gives a simple litmus test that I've found helpful in determining whose influence we choose to remain under.

Jesus said that His sheep know His voice and that the voice of a stranger they'll not follow (John 10:5, 27-28). The stranger is the god of this world. The strangers are the things and influencers that try to pull us away from righteousness.

Jesus also said, "But why do you call Me 'Lord, Lord,' and not do the things which I say?" (Luke 6:46).

Ouch, right? Does the Lord God have a say in your life? Do you give Him an opportunity to weigh-in? Is He allowed to influence your behavior?

When I started out with God, I'd been trained in the world under Satan's influence. I had to learn God's voice and His way. The number one way we get to know His voice is by spending time with Him reading the Bible. I didn't start out knowing what the Lord said. The more I grew spiritually, the more automatic right choices became.

And still, I don't do everything perfectly. But I endeavor to. I don't choose to listen to the voice of the stranger. I make a conscious decision to identify with God, not with the devil. I choose God's ways. Sometimes that just means, shut your mouth, Toni!

PAUL'S TESTIMONY

Before Christ, Paul said that he considered himself the chief of sinners (1 Timothy 1:15). After receiving Jesus as His Lord and Savior, he was no longer a slave and prisoner of Satan. He could walk worthy before God and keep the devil under his feet. Paul got it. He pleaded with the church to do the same.

He knew that without God's power working in us, our armor would do us no good. We're no match for the devil's wiles. That's why we need Holy Spirit's help to change our thinking to agree with God's way of thinking and doing life.

We all know many of God's kids who have died prematurely or who continue to live in lack and illness. If God was fighting all our battles like some proclaim, that makes the devil look bigger, stronger, and more powerful than God. That's just not true.

The devil has always known Jesus is more than he could ever hope to be, or handle. John 1:3 reminds us that Jesus has always existed. Satan knew Jesus in heaven.

God said, "And I will put enmity Between you and the woman, and between your seed and her Seed; **He** shall bruise your head, and you shall bruise His heel" (Genesis 3:15 emphasis mine).

Satan knew well who He was and is. Satan knew he couldn't take Him. That's why he killed so many babies around the birth of Jesus. He was trying to destroy the body Jesus arrived in.

OUR BEHAVIOR

Paul set his sights on "the high calling in Christ Jesus (Philippians 3:14). He chose to forget the mistakes he made and not to dwell on his failures. Paul tells us that we're to grow up and stop acting like children (Ephesians 4:14-15).

The clincher to staying fully dressed is found in Ephesians 4:22-23. This is something Paul says we're to do. This isn't something God comes in and does for us. He will help us. It describes our responsibility.

"Strip yourselves of your former nature [put off and discard your old unrenewed self] which characterized your previous manner of life and becomes corrupt through lusts and desires that spring from delusion; And be constantly renewed in the spirit of your mind [having a fresh mental and spiritual attitude]" (AMPC).

The only way to strip ourselves from the effects that our old nature holds over us is to renew our minds by reading and practicing the Word of God.

We need Holy Spirit for that. Instead of quenching Him we must learn to rely on His power that God made available to us. We must learn how to tap that power, or it'll be like having a coffee pot that doesn't have a power source attached. No coffee.

No coffee is serious business in my house. But not near as serious as having offended Holy Spirit.

Beginning with Ephesians 4:15, Paul talks about our behavior. He tells us to grow up and walk in love toward others. That's a heart matter. We're not to act and live like we're heathens under the influence of the god of this world. Heathens are perverse, full of folly, vain and futile in their minds and souls. The more we allow God's Word's to soak into us, the more we'll come under God's influence.

Strip to Stay Dressed

If we don't want to meet the devil naked, we strip ourselves of his nature.

For instance, anger is dangerous. If we're not careful it can lead to rage in a split second. Coach Paul told us to deal with anger before the sun goes down so that the devil doesn't gain an advantage over us (Ephesians 4:26). Anger penetrates our godly nature and is deadly.

Paul also told anyone who was stealing to knock it off and make an honest living. In other words, get a job, pal.

We're not supposed to use foul language. You may have cussed like you just ditched Folsom Prison, but you're the one who has to remove that life from your heart, mind and mouth. It'll stalk you like a wolf stalks his prey if you don't.

Make a godly choice to only allow good and encouraging words to come from your mouth.

Tough one? If I can do it you can do it! Whenever you mess up just ask God to forgive you and get right back on track as if nothing had happened.

Paul also tells us not to grieve, offend, or sadden Holy Spirit (Ephesians 4:30). Without Him, we'll fail. Holy Spirit is our source of strength and power. We may be sealed and headed for heaven one day, but we need His involvement in our daily lives.

Paul says we're not to allow bitterness, indignation, wrath, resentment, quarreling or slander. These things are not godliness characteristics.

"Let all bitterness and indignation *and* wrath (passion, rage, bad temper) and resentment (anger, animosity) and quarreling (brawling, clamor, contention) and slander (evil-speaking, abusive or blasphemous language) be banished from you, with all malice (spite, ill will, or baseness of any kind). And become useful *and* helpful *and* kind to one another, tenderhearted (compassionate, understanding, loving-hearted), forgiving one another [readily and freely], as God in Christ forgave you" (Ephesians 4:31-32 AMPC).

Why? First, because God said so. Second, these characteristics don't reflect our new nature of righteousness. Third, these behaviors and attitudes attract demonic activity. Attitudes and behaviors contrary to God's character open doors to the devil and leave us powerless.

God sees us as righteous, therefore we are. There's no condemnation here. You can act and talk anyway you choose. God will still love you, but it may cost you some battles. Winning warriors are disciplined in the ways of God.

The God life isn't easy, breezy. Being more than a conqueror through Christ takes discipline. Nothing is automatic. Begin where you are and start acting like God instead of the devil. God gave us permission to act like Him.

"Therefore, be imitators of God [copy Him *and* follow His example], as well-beloved children [imitate their father]. And walk in love, [esteeming and delighting in one another] as Christ loved us and gave Himself up for us, a slain offering and sacrifice to God [for you, so that it became] a sweet fragrance" (Ephesians 5: 1-2 AMPC).

As you can see, Paul had a lot to say before he wrote, "Finally, my brethren…" (Ephesians 6:10).

Being strong in the Lord and in the power of His might requires that we stay dressed in the whole armor of God.

Now that we understand how to keep our armor on, in *Never Meet the Devil Half Naked*, we'll talk about Ephesians 6:13. "Therefore take up the whole armor of God, that you may be able to withstand in the evil day, and having done all, to stand."

CHAPTER 15
Dear Daisy

The best advice I can give you is to just start living this God-life where you are.

That's what I did. I was full of the devil's behaviors. But I was willing to do things God's way and discovered that He only asked for a willing heart.

With Holy Spirit's help, I renewed my mind, and put on godliness.

I still miss the mark. Everyone does. Just don't practice messing up on purpose. When you mess up, be quick to repent and get back on track with the Son.

Ask Holy Spirit for His help and guidance. It may be a new thing, but you're capable of being led by Holy Spirit. Knowing God's Truth comes from spending time with Him reading the Bible.

Warriors live godly lives. We monitor our behavior towards God, others, and ourselves.

You are called to be a warrior. You can do it. You are called to be the best and most marvelous at living the God life. You have the ability within to win every battle and never meet the devil naked.

Until we meet again. It's time, Daisy. Arise.

Obtaining Your Armor

Before we receive the gift of God's faith and His armor, we need to receive Jesus, as our Lord and Savior.

The first step to becoming a warrior is to come to Jesus. If you've never received Jesus as the Lord of your life, or if you're not sure that you're what the Bible calls born-again—come to Jesus now. Maybe you'd like to come to Him and recommit your life to doing things His way.

Paul, under the guidance of Holy Spirit wrote, "For 'whoever calls on the name of the LORD shall be saved'" (Romans 10:13).

It's that simple. Salvation isn't a reward for doing everything right. Receiving your new nature is received by believing and calling out to the Lord. The Apostles preached the Word of Faith. We have Paul's testimony of that to the Romans.

"But what does it say? "The word is near you, in your mouth and in your heart" (that is, the word of faith which we preach): **that if you confess with your mouth the Lord Jesus and believe in your heart that God has raised Him from the dead, you will be saved"** (Romans 10:8-9 emphasis mine).

Notice in the last sentence that Paul said it's with the heart that one believes. If you can't speak, then write your declaration of belief on a piece of paper and believe it from your heart.

Write or call out to God. Say out loud, "God, I believe in my heart, and I confess with my mouth that Jesus is the Son of God who came in the flesh. I believe that He died in my place and that You raised Him from the dead. I believe that by His stripes I am healed now. I believe I am now your child. I am saved and born again by your Holy Spirit. I believe you are a forgiver and forgetter of sins. I ask you to forgive me of all my sins that are known and unknown to me. Take my life and teach me your ways."

God doesn't lie. If you believe in your heart and confess Jesus as your Lord with your mouth you are now His child. He says He blots out sin and chooses not to remember (Hebrews 8:12). He does this so that He can be close to you. Now trust Him.

Clothed with Holy Spirit

Often in life it seems we lack understanding or don't know how to pray. One of the gifts God gave us for that very purpose is Holy Spirit.

Holy Spirit comes to dwell in us when we're born again. There's also an additional experience that we're privileged to enjoy. It's called the baptism of the Holy Spirit. This is when we allow ourselves to be completely immersed in Him. The difference is that at salvation, He indwells us, and at the Baptism, we immerse ourselves in Him. When we give ourselves to Holy Spirit, He gives us a special prayer language called tongues. It's the language of the spirit and the devil can't understand it.

The only requirement for receiving Holy Spirit's baptism is that we're born again. If you'd like this special gift and prayer language, pray the prayer that follows.

Say out loud: *I am now reborn and Your child Father God. I ask You for the gift of the Holy Spirit. Holy Spirit immerse me with Yourself and rise up within me as I praise God. Thank You Father for the Holy Spirit. I expect to speak in other tongues as You give me the utterance.*

Now, lift your hands toward heaven as if you were a child and you wanted your Father to pick you up. Say thank You and start praising God for Holy Spirit. Praising God might sound something like this: *Father I thank you for Jesus. Thank you for sending Holy Spirit and giving me my prayer language. You are a wonderful Father. Thank you for loving me. You are so good to me. Halleluiah, halleluiah, halleluiah…*

Keep saying *halleluiah* with your own voice. As you sense an urge coming from your belly area to your vocal cords, allow yourself to give sound to whatever you sense. As you yield your tongue, you'll speak syllables and words that are not your natural language. They'll rise up and want release from your mouth. You have to use your own voice. You have to release the utterances the same as you'd release words in a conversation. Holy Spirit won't force you. It's a gentle nudge or prompting which you allow to rise and come out of your mouth.

Don't be concerned with how it sounds. Like with our babies, God's babies don't come with a full vocabulary. I only had three little syllables at first. The sounds you make are the language Holy Spirit gives you and it will develop as you practice—every day.

You are a born again, Spirit-filled believer. Your life will never be the same. Enjoy God's armor.

If you don't have a church, I encourage you to get in a good Bible believing church where you can learn and grow. Make sure they believe the full gospel and promote the power of Jesus Christ. Don't let anyone talk you out of what Father God wants to do in your life.

Acknowledgments

I am thankful for my warrior daughters, Tosha Miller and Fallon Pate. When God rescued me, He rescued my two little girls as well. Learning to live in the kingdom of God wasn't always easy. We had many challenges but look at us today! God did what God does. He forever changed our family's future and our destinies. I love you, Tosha and Fallon, with all my heart.

I am also thankful to my husband and mighty man of valor, John. I appreciate the years of encouragement and support as I endeavored to do the work God called me to do. I love you. There isn't anyone I'd rather do life with.

I count it a joy and a privilege to be part of Melanie Hemry's critique group. As my writing coach she's made my writing shine. As a friend, she's taught me to express God's compassion for others in the words I write. Thank you, Melanie, and thank you to my group's members. Each of you have had a role in shaping the writer in me. I appreciate your friendships.

Thank you to my friend and editor, Laurel Thomas, founder of *Write Your Heart Out*. I see your touch throughout the pages of this book. I appreciate my friend, Gloria Baumann and cousin, Corey Holloway. Both of you diligently reviewed every word of my manuscript. This is a better book because of the three of you.

I am grateful to my grandchildren. You inspire me. You motivate me. You encourage me. You keep me going. You make me smile and bring joy to my heart. Pouring into your lives to help you become all you're called to be in your generation, is my dessert. I love you all and I love being your Honey.

Notes

4. THE DEVIL'S STRATEGY

1. Rick Renner, *Dressed to Kill*, (Tulsa, OK: Teach All Nations, 2007), 197.
2. Ibid. 198.
3. Ibid. 200.

6. IT CAN GET HOT

1. Spiros Zodhiates, Th.D. *The Complete Word Study New Testament, Word Study Series*, (Chattanooga, TN: AMG Publishers), "Buffet," 2852. 43.

7. IN CHRIST

1. Marilyn Hickey
2. Noah Webster, "Redemption," *Webster's 1828 American Dictionary of the English Language, Compact Edition,* ((West Valley City, UT, Waking Lion Press, 2010), 672.

11. THE WARRIOR WITHIN

1. Rick Renner, *Sparkling Gems from the Greek*, (Tulsa, OK: Teach All Nations, 2003), 919.

13. GODLINESS

1. Noah Webster, "Godliness," (Entry 1) *Webster's 1828 American Dictionary of the English Language, Compact Edition,* ((West Valley City, UT, Waking Lion Press, 2010), 376.
2. Ibid. 694.
3. Ibid. 895.

About the Author

Ask **Toni Chism** what she does, she'll smile and answer, "I work for God."

Beginning her marketplace ministry, Toni purchased Bibles at garage sales and gave them to those she shared Jesus with. Today, she leads women into a position of spiritual strength so they can receive everything Jesus died to give.

Word of Faith Warrior, certified Advanced Christian Life Coach, international speaker, teacher and author, Toni has a bachelor's degree in journalism. She's authored articles, short stories and resources that have appeared in newspapers, magazines and books. She's the winner of the prestigious 2019 WriterCon Inspirational Writing Contest.

The wife of John, Toni lives in Oklahoma, drinks domestic coffee and writes from her log cabin in the woods that John planted for her. She has two daughters and eight grandchildren who call her Honey.

You can register for news, book release dates and more by opting-in on her email registry. Toni doesn't like her inbox bombarded and she'll never overload yours.

Visit Toni at www.tonichism.com.

SPIRITUAL WARFARE IS NOT A DRILL.

It's time to armor-up.

Download your FREE Spiritual Warrior Strategy at ToniChism.com.

Made in the USA
Coppell, TX
28 February 2022